ROBERT BURNS

HIS ASSOCIATES AND
CONTEMPORARIES

ROBERT BURNS
HIS ASSOCIATES AND CONTEMPORARIES

The Train, Grierson, Young, and Hope
Manuscripts, *Edited, with an Introduction*

BY

ROBERT T. FITZHUGH

WITH

THE JOURNAL OF THE BORDER TOUR

Edited by

DeLANCEY FERGUSON

CHAPEL HILL
The University of North Carolina Press
1943

To

D. W. F.

PREFACE

It is hoped that publication in full of the documents in this volume will make it easier to understand the man Burns was and was not. Professor Ferguson has most generously contributed the first complete text of the Journal of the Border Tour. To Mr. William Angus, Keeper of the Registers and Records of Scotland and custodian of the Grierson papers, I am indebted for access to those papers and for permission to publish them. And without the gracious leave of the Chancellor and the Principal of the University of Edinburgh, who allowed me to include the Train, Hope, and Young MSS, the volume could not have come into existence. Nor can I permit John McVie, Secretary of the Burns Federation, to remain the silent partner in this enterprise which his generous nature would prefer. It was he who first called my attention to the Grierson papers and who lent me invaluable aid in transcribing them. Finally, my special gratitude is due Professor C. B. Hale, of the University of Maryland, for reading and criticizing my manuscript.

The Train, Hope, Young, and Grierson MSS have all been reproduced as exactly as print and human frailty

allow, but it should be mentioned that in the interpreta-
tion of capital letters, particularly "K," "P," and "S" in
Young, in the choice of dash or period, in the recording
of such abbreviations as "Mr." and "Edinr.," and in the
placing of apostrophes in Young, it has often been necessary to act fairly arbitrarily. MS eccentricities possibly
attributable to editorial laxity have been marked " (sic) ,"
but here, too, consistency has been difficult.

R. T. F.

Works frequently mentioned have been abbreviated in
the notes as follows:

Robert Chambers, revised by William Wallace, *The Life
and Works of Robert Burns,* Edinburgh, 1896, 4 vols.
(Referred to as Ch-W).

DeLancey Ferguson, *The Letters of Robert Burns,* Oxford,
1931, 2 vols. (Referred to as Ferguson; the italicized
number in each reference is that of the letter, and the
following roman and arabic numbers are those of the
volume and page.)

W. E. Henley and T. F. Henderson, *The Poetry of Robert
Burns,* London, 1896, 4 vols. (Referred to as H&H).

CONTENTS

I
INTRODUCTION

I

—————

Robert Burns
His Tradition and His Work

What sort of man was Robert Burns? His birth, the paradox of his position, the richly embroidered tradition of his career as tavern drinker and amorist at large, his buoyant youthful defiance of convention, kirk, and king (especially when they interfered with his pleasures), his good humor and good fellowship—all these, together with the pathos of his early death, brought him blazing publicity in his own time. And, while only Scots now read much of Burns, and they the wrong poems and for the wrong reasons, the world is still fascinated by the man.

His reputation suffers yet from his early biographers. The first, Dr. Currie, felt the need to "gloss over his failings," and too many others wrote in the spirit of an unidentified critic who proclaimed in an obituary notice, "Let others profit by the misconduct of Burns." A nineteenth-century ferment of reticence, piety, sentiment, and imagination passed for Burns scholarship until William E. Henley protested the "tame, proper, figmentary" Burns which had been raised in the popular mind. Roundly abused for his pains by what he called "common Burnsites," Henley presented Burns not as an ignorant genius who burst inexplicably into great poetry, but as a man of more than common reading who worked in a well-established poetic tradition; not as a "proper, mid-Victorian journalist," but as a racy, salty, masculine countryman with immense gusto and a shrewd, not to say Rabelaisian, eye for men and their ways; not as a gross sinner who had miraculously produced fine poetry and tender songs, but as a man of tempestuous passions, who, ironically, rose to greatness in large measure because of them. He admitted much in Burns' life that one cannot admire. Burns did not admire it himself. A man in considerable measure does as he must and not as he will. Furthermore, we should note Professor Ferguson's remark that Burns was not so much a conspicuous sinner as one who sinned conspicuously. Scholarship and a more candid and tolerant public have come to agree with Henley that Burns as he lived, if not so satisfying to romantic piety, is better than Burns interpreted by reverent Victorian biographers.

During his first two decades, Burns seemed merely another intelligent young farmer in meager circumstances and with a taste for books, but by his early twenties he was already distinguished in his neighborhood, as he now is in the world, for satiric wit, humor, sentiment; for assertive self-confidence and a desire to shock and startle; for love of company and free talk; and for love of women. We have early accounts of his discomfiting his elders in churchyard theological disputes, of his making farm hands roll in a furrow and yell with laughter at his jokes, of his founding and dominating a village debating club—no Y. M. C. A., incidentally, of his gorging himself with sentimental poetry and fiction, of his easy approach with girls, and of the disapproval he stirred among the staider members of the community, who remarked that young Burns seemed to have a good deal to say for himself. Consciousness at once of his own superiority, of the world's absurdities, and of certain restraints society imposed on him, made Burns cocky and defiant, and urged him to seek the company of other high-spirited youngsters similarly disposed, and to write such poems as his wholly delightful "Welcome to a Bastart Wean." Throughout his life he continued this taste for boisterous and jovial good-fellowship, often over a glass, but neither early nor late did he become a drunkard. In later years he had more time and more money to indulge this taste, and it certainly did his health, ruined by hard work at fifteen, no good. But in hard-drinking eighteenth-century Scotland, Burns was not notable for excess. On the other hand, his love for women brought him by his own statement eleven illegitimate children, four of them (two pairs of twins) by Jean Armour, whom he later married, and who subsequently bore him three sons and a daughter. Comment here is superfluous. However, he is a strict moralist who would wish away the songs and poems celebrating Burns' heroines, and the heroines wished it least of all. One wrote in her diary on the fortieth anniversary of her parting with him, "This day I can never forget. Parted with Burns, in the year 1791, never more to meet in this world. Oh, may we meet in Heaven!" Another, asked in her old age if she remembered nights among the rigs of barley with him, answered with a twinkle, "Aye, brawlie that!" And his own wife remarked with unique authority, "Our Robert should have had two wives." There let the matter rest. It plagued him enough while alive.

For one who indulged himself in reckless self-assertion, Burns was peculiarly vulnerable. He had neither the thick skin to ignore inevitable retaliations, nor the heavy purse to disdain them. But he would not learn wisdom, and in

consequence he met continued rebuffs and worse.   When
he had suffered a galling public rebuke in church for his
illegal paternity of Betty Paton's child, the laughter that
followed his satirical shots at Church Quarrels, Holy Fairs,
Holy Willies, and "practical bigotry" in general, was at
least partial satisfaction.   And one feels a natural sympathy with him.   But what can one say of his answering
an Edinburgh hostess he had not met that he would be
glad to accept her invitation if she would also invite the
Learned Pig, then being exhibited for money? Despite his
wit we are not surprised that after several such incidents,
Edinburgh society dropped him.   Nor need we wonder that
he made no faster progress in the King's service.   Had he
not written on a tavern window the following comment on
the reigning king, George III, and his family:

> An idiot race, to honor lost—
> Who know them best despise them most?

Here again, truth, wit, and personal irritation are com-
bined prettily, as they had been in his attacks on the Kirk,
but without any of the provocation, and with the marked
difference that Burns was now a national figure whose
words were given instant circulation.   Even less could he
now afford the satisfaction of attacks which gratified passing
resentments than he could as the Rantin' Dog of Mossgiel
Farm, particularly when the resentment was trivial and the
attack dangerous.   But Burns not only failed to curb his
spleen; he spoke as though the ill will he generated were
largely the hard lot of native genius under a class system.
"A man's a man for a' that," he cried; the upper classes
grind the lower, who share at least common humanity with
them.   It is particularly hard for low-born merit to achieve
recognition and reward, and particularly galling to see
well-born dullness and insolence preferred.   Truth, every

word, and honor to him for saying it so movingly. But what of that overflow of the same sentiment which made him propose the following toast to officers in the king's army, "May the last king be hanged in the guts of the last priest?"

One cannot understand Burns or his poetry until he grasps this paradox: his cry for liberty was sharpened by his impatience with restraint; his democracy was more than tinged with resentment of his superiors, and often of the ill will he himself had stirred up unprovoked. His readiness, his wit, his humor were often embittered by too much of the same sense of the world's injustice and hypocrisy and absurdity that gives zest to his poems. The "head-long passions" and "skinless sensibility" that prompted his best poetry also drove him to excesses and outbursts of which no one can be proud. His own lines may be poor apology, but they are simple truth:

> The light that led astray
> Was light from heaven.

A further paradox is that although his birth and position hampered him and created prickly situations in which his sensitive pride made him writhe and occasionally strike, his fame as a poet is mainly due to his wisdom in avoiding a false gentility in his life and in his art, and in writing of the life he knew, in its own fast-fading dialect of which he was master, and in the spirit of a well-established vernacular tradition.

That a clever young Ayrshire farmer in 1780 should have tried his hand at Scots verse is no such great wonder as is often supposed. Burns says of himself, as though it were nothing unusual, that he was "just a rhymer like by chance," one of a common class. His own village boasted three vernacular rhymers, himself, Saunders Tait, a tailor, and David Sillar, a farm boy like Burns. John Lapraik, of a neighboring village, was another, and many more, like William Simpson, Janet Little, and Symon Gray, crossed Burns' path. Nor has the tradition of village rhymers died out today; J. Leslie Mitchell, in a recent novel of Scots village life, included a rhymer as a typical character, and a volume of poems by Burns' great-grandson, Robert Burns Thomson, published in Winnipeg in 1937, attests the urge to rhyme even in Scots transplanted to Western Canada.

Indeed, the wonder is not that Burns followed this tradition and hitched his feelings into rhyme, but that his rhymes were poetry. For there was little in the Scots Vernacular in 1780 to suggest that a great poet would ever again use it as his vehicle. A court language in Henryson and Dunbar's time, the Vernacular in Burns' day was spoken, in a variety of dialects such as his own Ayrshire, mainly by the lower classes. It was still, with an admixture of English, a conventional language of songs and ballads, and of a considerable body of popular humorous poetry and magazine verse; but during the century or more before Burns, with a few exceptions, literary Scots had been trying to write English, and the Scotch public had been supplied largely with English poetry and fiction. Burns spoke English and wrote excellent English prose, and he was thoroughly familiar with English literature of the eighteenth century, but when he attempted verse in the style of that period, he was hopelessly wooden. Success required a finesse of which he confessed himself incapable.

He turned instinctively to the traditional stanzas and forms of familiar vernacular verse, writing of his local scene in a mixture of Scots and English, the latter often couched in the incongruous eighteenth-century formal poetic diction. He confessed his advantage in having two languages from which to choose words and rhymes, and it is not so much his language as his subjects and spirit and style which mark him as a vernacular poet. Homely realism, jocular good humor, sentiment, homespun satire and reflection, and songs to sing, these were, for his day, traditional vernacular media. In them the effects were free and broad, and not comparable to those of the carefully wrought couplets and stanzas of Young and Shenstone and Goldsmith and Gray, all of whom Burns admired and laid under tribute.

But even as the English poets inherited the tradition of Waller and Dryden and Pope, and a public ear attuned to wit, morality, and the couplet, so did Burns inherit forms and subjects, a style and a public. And his achievement is the more remarkable in that he had no great predecessors to show the way. Even the two men from whom he learned most, Allan Ramsay and particularly Robert Fergusson, though they wrote skillful, racy vernacular poetry well above the level of that by village rhymers, were both, like those rhymers, of chiefly local and contemporary interest. In the Vernacular they wrote mainly of eighteenth-century Edinburgh, its customs and peculiar flavor, poems still choice, but of limited appeal and interesting mainly as the models from which Burns worked.

Their and Burns' verse forms, the tetrameter couplet of "The Twa Dogs" and "Tam o' Shanter," the involved bob-wheel stanza of the "Epistle to Davie," the eight-line stanza with a refrain of "The Holy Fair," and the famous six-line stave built on two rhymes, which Burns found most congenial, these were the common heritage of all Scots vernacular poets. And so were the subjects and patterns of the twenty-five or thirty poems which made Burns' reputation and which sustain it. For, while his dialogues, addresses, epistles, descriptions of popular gatherings and customs, and humorous poems occasioned by the real or presumed death of the victim, all derive from similar poems in Ramsay and Fergusson, Ramsay's and Fergusson's in turn derived from such poems as "Christ's Kirk o' the Green" and "Peebles to the Play" (racy descriptions of village merrymaking like "Hallowe'en," "The Holy Fair," and "The Jolly Beggars") ; as "The Epitaph of Habbie Simpson, Piper of Kilbarchan" (prototype of gusty comic elegies like Tam Samson's); and as "The Last Dying Words of Bonnie Heck, a famous Grey-hound in the Shire of Fife" (original of many a predecessor to Burns' "unco mournfu' tale" of poor Maillie) .

In the last two genres, Ramsay produced "Lucky Spence's Last Advice," a famous bawd's parting words to her charges, and comic elegies to both Maggy Johnstoun, brewer of excellent ale, and John Cowper, an assistant kirk treasurer, part of whose official duty it was to apprehend Edinburgh prostitutes in the name of religion and public morals; while Fergusson wrote a moving elegy to his professor of mathematics at Saint Andrews, who

> cou'd divine,
> Whan he did read
> That *three* times *three* just made up nine;
> But now he's dead.

In these and in such descriptions of popular holiday making as Ramsay's continuation of "Christ's Kirk o' the Green" and Fergusson's "Hallow-fair," "Leith Races," and "The Daft-Days" (Christmas and New Year holidays) , Burns found not only subjects and hints for developing them, but the way to use poverty and low life picturesquely and with broad good humor. Much the same tone of homespun joviality also marked the versified epistles of Ramsay and Lieutenant William Hamilton of Gilbertfield, which are the basis of Burns' famous epistles to Davie and Smith and Lapraik. In these loosely joined, personal poems on a variety of topics, Ramsay and Hamilton assumed the character, which Burns also adopted, of boon companions who exchanged jocular criticism and compliment and who sealed their friendship over a bowl.

In both Ramsay and Fergusson and elsewhere, Burns found topics and forms, tricks of phrase and points of style. But, aside from some suggestions in Fergusson, the qualities in his poems that continue to move us are almost wholly lacking in the best vernacular verse from which he took his bearings. In Fergusson's work alone is there much more than a keen eye for amusing detail and interest in humorous situation. In him there is zest for the human comedy and sympathetic interest in man's struggles, and hopes, and achievements, and even ludicrous failures. Moreover, Burns found in Fergusson something of the spirit that later guided him in the famous lines describing Tam o' Shanter at the inn:

> Ae market-night,
> Tam had got planted unco right,
> Fast by an ingle, bleezing finely,
> Wi' reaming swats, that drank divinely;
> And at his elbow, Souter Johnie,
> His ancient, trusty, drouthy cronie:
> Tam lo'ed him like a very brither;
> They had been fou for weeks thegither.
> The night drave on wi' sangs and clatter;
> And ay the ale was growing better:
> The landlady and Tam grew gracious
> Wi' secret favours, sweet and precious:
> The Souter tauld his queerest stories;
> The landlord's laugh was ready chorus:
> The storm without might rair and rustle,
> Tam did na mind the storm a whistle.

Fergusson never achieved that brilliant combination of sympathetic humor, rich detail, varied movement, and pointed phrase, but he came near it, and Burns owed him a heavy debt he was ever quick to acknowledge.

For Burns, like that other famous country boy, from Stratford village, accepted as models the successful work of others, and then garnished his own poetry with shrewder understanding, and richer humor and imagination, and, greatest of all, with a masterly grasp and authoritative language that gives it a continued vitality when the models are faded and forgotten. And, unlike Shakespeare's, Burns' work breathes a striking and buoyant personality, which is perhaps its greatest charm. We must remember all this when we come to estimate his achievement. Moreover, we must come to see that Burns was no heaven-taught ploughman or isolated phenomenon. And though, like the Romantics, he absorbed contemporary sentimentalism with its doctrine of man's individual dignity and rights, and though he wrote personal poetry of rich emotional content, the most fruitful criticism of his work can come from regarding him not as a "Romantic" at all, but as the last great figure of the earthy, racy, and not infrequently bawdy Scots Vernacular Tradition.

By a curious paradox, however, if one seeks in Burns that tradition at its best, uncontaminated by eighteenth-century formal diction and by sentimentalism, he will savor it most fully in poems for which Burns found few direct hints—in his satires, particularly "Holy Willie's Prayer," and in his verse tale, "Tam o' Shanter." There, and in the "recitatives" of "The Jolly Beggars," free from personalities and class consciousness, Burns has embroidered brilliant description and colorful, dramatic narrative with broad and gusty humor, in the fullest extension of his powers and the widest expression of his genius.

"Tam o' Shanter" stands unique in Burns and in our literature, and it is easily one of the few great poems of its century. Its humor, and rapid variety of scene, and vivid detail, and the compelling sweep and zest of the story make it so wholly delightful that comment but stales its infinite variety. It must be read and heard. And of Burns' satire it must be said that in no other English or Scotch satirist with Burns' keen eye and deadly thrust, is there the same overwhelming good humor and almost sympathy with the victim. Dr. Hornbook, the village quack (whom, later, by the way, Burns helped with a substantial loan), is laughed down with a burst of friendly derision that completely destroys him, and yet did not destroy his friendship with Burns. Similarly in his "Address to the Deil," Burns jokes the Devil completely out of his Calvinist Hell, which, he says, is no place even for a Devil. But greatest of all is "Holy Willie's Prayer," that "amazing achievement in satire—so nice, so exquisite in detail, so overwhelming in effect," in which Willie's outraged conscience seeks divine consolation for indignities suffered as God's vicar in Mauchline parish.[1]

For those who find this side of Burns not to their taste, there are his songs in which they will find what they almost certainly want, sentiment. The deliberate appeal to emotions, with conscious artifice and distortion of values, was

[1] An aftermath of this pious event deserves to be better known. Upon the authority of Thomas Kennedy, who had become his fellow townsman in Cortland, New York, Henry S. Randall, in *The Knickerbocker* of March, 1836, relates how Burns revealed to Willie that his prayer had been overheard. Urged by Burns, Kennedy invited Willie to enjoy "a bit o' satire" on a distinguished local elder, on condition he should hear it through without speaking. The victim accepted with a relish that was heightened by the first few stanzas, but by the seventh he broke his promise and roared, "That blackguard Burns!," and at the eighth, rushed from the room, exclaiming, "That blackguard Burns!—he'll go to hell—he'll go to hell!"

a sophisticated element in eighteenth-century literature that seduced Burns' "skinless sensibility." Too often his sentiment is false and forced, or, what is worse, it is a self-conscious savoring of itself. Even such widely and deservedly popular poems as those to a mouse and to a mountain daisy reek with overcharged benevolence and carefully calculated appeals to our tender feelings; and they both close on a note of conscious self-pity. Moreover, we should note the essential falseness of Burns' feeling any mouse his "poor earth-born companion an' fellow mortal," and particularly *his* comparing the daisy's fate to that

> of artless maid,
> Sweet flow'ret of the rural shade!
> By love's simplicity betray'd,
>   And guileless trust;
> Till she, like thee, all soil'd is laid
>   Low i' the dust.

Pious humanitarianism, embellished with vivid detail, is still popular, and the line between sentiment and sentimentality is not sharp, but a comparison of these poems with "The Twa Dogs" or "The Auld Farmer's New-Year Morning Salutation to his Auld Mare, Maggie" reveals at once the difference between warm human feeling delicately caught, and pumped-up, artificial display.

If one wishes, he can find in Burns, particularly in the songs, sentiment that is true and clear and fine and tender. For instance, the varieties of love: a girl's shyness, her difficulty in deciding between two lovers, her hopeful and desperate faith in her lover just before her baby is to be born, her meditating proper decorum on meeting a lad while comin' thro' the rye, all these and many more he catches perfectly. Drinking songs, humorous songs, pathetic songs, patriotic songs—he has left superb examples of them all. And he furnished the English-speaking world with its universal, if not always understood, song to celebrate old times remembered, old friendships renewed, and present friends and pleasures to be cherished. The tune and at least some of the words of "Auld Lang Syne" are as familiar to all of us as our beds. And perhaps this would have been the achievement most pleasing to Burns.

For he was one of the few men of his time who took a serious interest in the folk songs of Scotland. In his travels, on his excise rounds, by correspondence, and through every means open to him, he made heroic efforts to collect all the songs of his country and to find or compose decent words for them. And it should be remembered that Burns wrote his words to music and intended them to be sung. He came at a time when popular native songs were fast disappearing either into limbo or the collections of antiquarians, and had it not been for him they might well have died altogether. As it was, he fitted fragments together, built new songs around a phrase or stanza, revised here and retouched there, until single-handed he had literally restored Scots song to life, and had left at least two score of the finest lyrics in the world.

And this during years when he was working at the uncongenial excise, when his society was either patronizing country gentry or small-town tradesmen and worse, when his health was failing, and when his hopes were dimming for a comfortable living and time for poetry while he still had poetry in him. Conscious that for him brilliant prospects had opened only briefly, and had not been fulfilled, he knew his genius and the driving energy behind it had largely wasted themselves away; nor was the knowledge comforting, and he sought consolation where he could find it.

Finally, however, careless living and hard work, particularly the latter, caught up with him, and his heart, early overstrained, showed signs of failure. Much enfeebled by a long illness, his wife expecting a baby, his debts pressing him, his death fairly certain in his own mind, Burns took the advice of his doctors and went to the seaside for a rest, and for "seabathing," in the hope that he would improve. The place he went to was no gay resort with a bright, sandy beach, but a remote hamlet on a bleak and sedgy shore of the Solway Firth. And there, removed from his friends and family, almost entirely alone, Burns sat day after day under a hawthorne tree and saw his strength gradually slip away. Each afternoon he waded out until the cold water came up to his armpits, and then waded back to sit under the hawthorne again and think of his daily more apparent end. And, after he had become entirely certain the end was not far off, he climbed wearily into a carriage and was driven back to Dumfries.

His friends at once came to see him, and were shocked at the evident nearness of his death. One of them wrote another:

"My dear Cunningham

I wrote you last Sunday and mentioned that our friend Burns was very ill—I conceive it to be a task (you would not forgive me did I omit it) to mention now, that I believe it is all over with him. I am this minute come from the mournful chambers in which I have seen the expiring genius of Scotland departing with Burns. Dr. Maxwell told me yesterday he had no hopes—today the hand of death is visibly fixed upon him. I cannot dwell on the scene—It overpowers me—yet Gracious God were it in thy power to recover him! He had life enough to acknowledge me—and

Mrs. Burns said he had been calling on you and me continually—He made a wonderful exertion when I took him by the hand—with a strong voice he said, 'I am much better today,—'I shall be soon well again for I command my spirits & my mind. But yesterday I resigned myself to death'—Alas it will not do—"

And it did not do. Within two days Burns was dead. Dumfries gave him a fine funeral; his friends got up a sub-scription for the widow; and his critics began a chorus that still continues. But to most of us now, "it is history that, while there was an infinite deal of the best sort of good in Burns, the bad in him, being largely compacted of such purely unessential defects as arrogance, petulance, imprudence, and a turn for self-indulgence, this last exasperated by the conditions in which his lot was cast, was not of the worst kind after all."[2] Yet these more vivid qualities have obscured his generous family loyalty, his responsibility as a husband and his affectionate concern as a father, his sturdy acceptance of inevitable hard work and distasteful duties, his patriotism, his quixotic honesty and integrity, and his abhorrence of cant and pettiness. But however the emphasis is laid, Burns' life stands before us as by no means an ignoble passage redeemed by genius. And it is ever more clear that John Syme's vision was prophetic when he saw "the expiring genius of Scotland departing with Burns."

[2] W. E. Henley, "Robert Burns: Life, Genius, Achievement," *Centenary Burns* (London and Edinburgh, 1896), Vol. IV.

The Significance of the Manuscripts

James Grierson and Joseph Train.—"Grierson is a curious old fellow.—He has been an enthusiastic collector of such matters connected with Burns for upwards of 20 years —during which time he has repeatedly visited the various places of the Poet's residences."[3] So wrote Joseph Train in 1828 of one who had given him information about Burns which he was forwarding to John Lockhart.[4] But partly because some of the stories in Train's memorandum were scandalous, and partly because "Grierson" was not identified further, the Train MS has remained unjustly suspect.

[3] Train MS, *post.*

[4] Joseph Train, native of Ayrshire, Supervisor of Customs at Dumfries and later at Castle Douglas, antiquarian, and friend of Sir Walter Scott, was an obvious person for John Lockhart to consult, perhaps through his father-in-law, about his Life of Burns. Whatever the medium, early in Chapter IX he acknowledges information just received, an obvious reference to the Train MS, ten sheets, 7½ x 9¾ in., written on one side, and now in the Library of the University of Edinburgh. Lockhart says, "Since the first pages of this narrative were sent to the press, I have heard from an old acquaintance of the bard, who often shared his bed with him at Mossgiel, that even at that early period, . . . it was his custom to have a great tub of water by his bedside. . . ." (*Life of Robert Burns*, Edinburgh, 1828. Vol. xxiii of *Constable's Miscellany*.)

However, recently uncovered notes[5] of James Grierson of Dalgoner[6] show him to have been the Grierson who supplied Train with material gleaned from reliable witnesses.[7] Much of it came from John Richmond, Burns' crony in 1786, 1787, and 1788, but he was by no means the only source. Those mentioned in the notes include John Blane, farm servant at Mossgiel; John Lambie, once Burns' ploughboy; one Hepburn of Kilmarnock, a friend of Tam Samson; "Mr. Carfrae, Printer, son of Mrs. Carfrae, Upper Baxter's Close Edinr with whom Richmond and Burns lodged"; David Sillar; Robert Ainslie; Agnes McLehose (Clarinda) ; A. C. McLehose, W. S., her son; and Mrs. James Anderson, Highland Mary's sister. Moreover, it is highly probable that these were not all, and that not all of Grierson's notes are now included in the papers at the Register House, for both Grierson and Train[8] mention items no longer to be found.

Conscientious but unsystematic, Grierson made his notes in a minute, ill-written hand on any convenient piece of paper, and seldom transcribed them. Ranging from mere scraps to full sheets, his papers are a chaotic mixture of items copied or clipped from newspapers, reports of interviews with those who had known Burns, drafts and proofs of letters to the editor, accounts of various affairs unconnected with Burns, transcripts of Burns' poems and letters,

[5] These notes are now in the custody of Mr. William Angus, Keeper of the Registers and Records of Scotland, H. M. Register House, Edinburgh, to whom I am indebted for the identification of their author.

[6] Near Dunscore, Dumfriesshire.

[7] Only five items (the "sonsie lass," Holy Willie, Farm of Mossgiel, The Armours, and Burns' Marriage), about which Train himself may have had personal information, are either unattributed to Grierson or without originals in the notes.

[8] Train MS, *post,* at the end, and reference to "The Trogger," Grierson Papers, IV.

and miscellaneous intelligence. Because most of the entries are scrupulously dated, it is possible to arrange them in chronological order, which reveals a sharp stimulation of Grierson's interest in 1814, followed by a period of active inquiry, especially in Ayrshire in 1817. In 1829 and 1830, after his connection through Train with Lockhart's Life, Grierson called upon Clarinda and her son, and Robert Ainslie.

What are the results for us of the Laird of Dalgoner's interest in Burns? A group of anecdotes, a glimpse of Burns' mother, two minor poems, a considerable body of information about his associates and contemporaries, the circumstances surrounding the composition of "To a Haggis," new light on the quarrel with Creech, and the most direct link with Highland Mary on record; these are surely no inconsiderable addition to our knowledge at this late date.

The Young and Hope Manuscripts.—Despite his evident Tory primness, Alexander Young, of Harburn, W. S., was a shrewd observer whose lively and varied recollections of Burns and Burns' contemporaries have too long remained in manuscript.[9] In addition to his account of Burns, perhaps the greatest interest lies in his remarks on Dr. Currie's opinion of Burns, and in those on William Nicol, Robert Riddell, Robert Heron, Lord Monboddo and his daughter, and John Syme, and also in his further evidence of Allan

[9] Both the Young and Hope manuscripts are now in the library of the University of Edinburgh. I owe my identifications and the photostats from which I have worked to the kindness of the Librarian, Mr. Lauriston Sharp. Young's rough draft fills both sides of twenty-five sheets 12 x 7½ in., his fair copy both sides of fifteen sheets the same size, his notes on Cunningham's eighth volume, beginning on the reverse of the last sheet of the fair copy, both sides of five more, and his account of the circumstances of the memoir three additional sides. The Hope memoir fills eleven sides of the same size.

Cunningham's editorial casualness. The present text is that of Young's fair copy, supplemented by variants and deletions from his rough draft, referred to as "r.d."[10] Both versions exhibit many discreet deletions.

The Hope memoir supplements Young's, and gives further light on upper-class opinion of Burns. It was written by the Right Honorable Charles Hope, later Lord Granton.

[10] His rough draft is dated 1834, and his fair copy, "Notes on Robert Burns omitted or Improved," 1835. This "principal Extended Copy [was] sent to Mr. J. G. Lockhart pr. Mr. Cadell" on May 16, 1837.

II
THE GRIERSON PAPERS

II

THE GRIERSON PAPERS

Grierson's Notes of 1805

The earliest marks of Grierson's interest in Burns are the items below, collected in 1805.

A. Part of a letter,[1] docketed "Burns to Baily Hill Edinr" and "got from Mr Stewart & compd with Baily Hill's original 22 June 1805."[2]

What are you doing & how are you doing. Have you lately seen any of my few friends—What is become of the Borough reform etc.[3]

[1] Ferguson, *387*, II, 6. Peter Hill was assistant to Creech, Burns' publisher. "Mr. Stewart" was probably Thomas Stewart, the Glasgow publisher, who in 1799 brought out "The Jolly Beggars" and other poems in a series of weekly tracts, and in 1801 collected them in a volume.

[2] On the reverse of this letter is Grierson's note: "Miss Burns, Matthews, was from Durham, her house was in Rose St. in the neighborhood of Lord Stonefield in her house was a Riot one night at which Lord S daughters took offense and raised a process to have her removed but decided, after being moved to the Court of Session in her favour, 12 Dec 1789 see Edin Mag 1789 p 88." The lady had originally been brought before Magistrate Creech, who gave her a severe sentence.

[3] Here a gap in the MS, filled with these notes: "Roslin, Durham Ld Swinton See Edin Mag v 10 Monthly Register p. 86 see Reliques 102 Elliesland 2 Feb 1790"

How is the fate of my poor name sake Mle Burns decided? Which of their Grave Lordships can lay his hand on his heart & say—that he has not taken the advantage of such frailty? Nay if we may judge by near 6m years experience—can the world do without such Frailty—Oh Man! but for the (sic) & thy selfish appetites & dishonest artifices—that beauteous form—& that once innocent & still ingenous (sic) Mind Might have shone conspicuous & lovely in the faithful wife & the affectionate Mother, & shall the unfortunate sacrifice to thy pleasures—have no claim to thy humanity!! As for those flinty bosom'd puritani[c] prosecutors of female frailty & persecutors of female charms.

I am quite sober—I am dispassionate—to shew you that I am so—I shall mend my pen ere I proceed.

It is written "Thou shalt not take the name of the Lord thy God in vain" so I shall neither say God curse them nor God blast them—nor God damn them—but May woman blast them—May woman curse & damn them.[4] May her lovely hand inexorably shut—the portal of Rapture to their most earnest prayers & fondest essays for entrance, and when many years & much port & great business—have delivered them over to Vulture Gouts & Aspen Palsies—*then* may the dear bewitching charmer—in derision, throw open the blessed[5] gate—to tantalize their impotent desires—which like ghosts haunt their bosoms—When all their powers to give or receive enjoyment are forever asleep in the Sepulchres of their fore fathers.[6]

---

[4] Ferguson, "May Woman curse them! May Woman blast them! May Woman damn them!"

[5] Ferguson, "blissful."

[6] Ferguson, "fathers." Grierson adds, "The cause was finally given in favour of Miss Burns."

B. Three poems and three fragments.[7]

1. on a dog of Lord Eglintons

> I never barked when out of season
> I never bit without a reason
> I ne'er insulted weaker brother
>   Nor wronged by force or fraud another
> We brutes are placed a rank below
>   Happy for man could he say so.[8]

2. To the Memory of the Unfortunate Miss Burns
   1791

> Like to a fading flower in May
>   Which Gardner cannot save
> So Beauty must, sometime, decay
>   And drop into the grave
>
> Fair Burns for long the talk and toast
>   Of many a gaudy Beau
> That Beauty has forever lost
>   What made each bosom glow.
>
> Think fellow sisters on her fate
>   Think, think how short her days
> Oh! think & e'er it be too late
>   Turn from your evil ways
>
> Beneath this cold green sod lies dead
>   That once bewitching dame
> That fired Edina's lustful sons
>   And quench'd their glowing flame.

[7] Items 3, 4, and 6 are by Burns; the lines to Miss Burns are directly ascribed to him in the Train MS, and the Epigram on Lord Eglinton's Dog is in the style and spirit of "versicles" he was fond of producing. The Eglinton estate was a few miles from Mauchline, and a member of the family was one of Mary Campbell's patrons.

[8] The position of these lines, just below the letter to Hill and opposite a transcription of Stanza IV of "A Bard's Epitaph," suggests they were an additional, authentic tidbit offered Grierson by either Hill or Stewart.

3. No more of your titled acquaintances boast
    Nor of the gay groups you have seen
    A crab louse is but a crab louse at last
    Tho' stack to the   of a Queen.

4. Three lawyers' tongues turned inside out,
    Wi' lies seamed like a beggar's clout;
    Three Priest's hearts, rotten black as muck
    Lay stinking, vile, in every neuk.[9]

5. Lo worms enjoy the seat of bliss
    Where Lords & Lairds afore did kiss.

6. Stanza IV of "A Bard's Epitaph."

Notes of 1814-1817

A decade later, as Grierson read through Currie's Life, he jotted down forty-three queries,[10] largely about the identity of persons Burns knew or mentioned; and he must have secured most of the answers he recorded from John Richmond and others interviewed in the years subsequent to his reading Currie. Grierson's notes on Currie are interesting only for their date, June 4, 1814, which marks the fruitful revival of his interest in Burns that prompted the visits and interviews recorded below.

[9] Ornaments of the "haly table" later removed by Burns. H&H I, 440.

[10] The form of one, "What do you know of him," suggests Grierson was addressing someone (probably his correspondent, Richmond), but answers to several include references to pages in Currie where he obviously found the information himself. Although accurate, the fifteen answers Grierson set down, all but one connected with Ayrshire, add nothing to our knowledge and are omitted. Identification of Mrs. Merry (the heroine of "corn Rigs") and Mrs. Dunlop reappear in the Train MS.

A. Memorandum[11] of a conversation with John Blane.

Glasgow 15 June 1814

John Blane, (now driver of the Lord Nelson Coach from Kilmk to Cumnock) was farm servant to Burns during a part of his Lease of Mossgiel—as they slept during the night together he had opportunities of oberving (sic) the Poet in all circumstances—

J. B. sat beside Burns in church on the day when the Incident occured (sic) wh gave occasion to the Poem of the Louse, & was surprized when Burns awakened him, the middle of the same night, & repeated to him all the stanzas, requesting his opinion of them,—this was the most surprizing Proofs of the facility with which Burns composed, that Came within J. B.'s Knowledge—

In the laborious employment of husbandry, the Peculiarities of Burn's (sic) mind were easily discernable—While engaged in Thrashing, it was evident that his mind was particularly occupied, from the varied alternations from slow to quick wh rendered it dangerous & even impossible for another to Keep time with him but in an hour or two he was quite exhausted & gave in altogether.—

A simple occurrence commented on by Burns in his own commanding way, has never since failed to Impress this persons mind, in regard to Cruelty to animals. When walking together, J. B. having a whip in his hand, gave a slight touch of it at a sparrow, & deprived it of some of its feathers—Upon this occasion Burns made so solemn an appeal to his Conscience, upon the unnecessary & wanton barbarity of the action that he has Ever since been Influenced by his admonition to resist similar Temta-

[11] Occupying a single sheet, with Stanza IV of "A Bard's Epitaph" below it.

tions (*sic*) —Burns uniformly digested & arranged his Compositions mentally, before he committed them to paper—

B. Memoranda docketed "Notes[12] Machline 15 Aug 1817, by John Richmond, writer."

Mrs. Carfrae[13] upper Baxter's close   Burns & Richmond Lodgings
                [Land Market
North side Land Market west side   1787

John Lambie,[14] Thatcher, Stevenson, led the Plough when Burns turned up the mouse.

Simpson, Schoolmaster Cumnock, wrote the poem to Burns in the name of a Taylor at Ochiltree "ye lousy bitch to thrash my Back at sic a pitch"[15]

C. A proof or offprint with some corrections in Grierson's hand and three additional notes, also in his hand.

To the Editor of the Glasgow Chronicle
Sir:

I have been told and for many years believed, that our great poet Burns was born where the cottage now stands in

[12] Many have no connection with Burns. There is a group on extraordinary feats of memory, another group on "Mimickry," and one note on an excellent treatment for razor straps. The notes here quoted are interesting chiefly because they reappear in the Train MS, and because they illustrate Grierson's habit of following up his leads carefully. Items B, D, and E, with other, unrelated matter, fill both sides of a sheet.

[13] Grierson later called on Mrs. Carfrae's son.

[14] Grierson also called on Lambie.

[15] A visit to David Sillar on the way to Mauchline is recorded just below this note on Simpson: "13 [August] Called on Dav Sillar, Irvine, 'a brother poet' he read over his sermon & various pieces of his manuscript poetry, he read from a slate, part of a reply he was preparing to a letter from me requesting a history of himself & Misfortunes. his brother from whom he had large succession was in partnership with Mr Henderson & sillar from Orkney in an African house Walker in a rope making &."

which a painting of him is exhibited, the property of the Shoemakers of Ayr, and about a mile distant from that town.

But lately I have been assured that this was not the fact, that he was born while his father resided at Doonholmgate, and was gardiner (*sic*) to Provost Wm Fergusson of Doonholm; and that he did not build the far famed cottage till several summers after the birth of Robert. This I find confirmed by a poetic Taylor, who says he made our great poet's first short clothes, and also by one of his earliest friends now in life; and if we may judge by some of Burns' letters, not yet printed, or likely soon to be printed, one of the most attached; and, upon looking into his life, Currie's edition, p 37, himself says, "for the first six or seven years of my life my father was gardener to a worthy gentleman of small estate in the neighbourhood of Ayr;" but, still as these two places are not far distant it is possible the place where the painting is exhibited may be the true place of his birth. The probability is against it . . .

[There follows a plea for the desirability of settling this disputed point.]

Cairnensis, Dumfriesshire, Aug. 1817

1st Note   At Mauchline, Dumfries, etc. the particular room and inn are yet pointed out where Burns wrote such and such a poem; as the Poacher Court was wrote in the east room, upstairs, of Murray's Inn, Mauchline, formerly John Dows.

2d   While Burns was thrashing, etc. his companions had often much difficulty to keep pace with him, for he was often either slow or very quick, according to the state of his mind, his violence soon exhausted him, when he threw himself on the straw quite worn out.

3rd   When Burns was in Edinburgh, 1787, attending the first edition of his poems there he was asked to be of a party; he thought it was for the purpose of exhibiting, answered that he would, on condition they had also the learned pig present The performance of this animal was then exhibited in Edinburgh for money.

D. Miscellaneous Notes[16]

Oct. 1817

Tam Sampson was a Nursery man at Kilmarnock where that business was carried to a greater extent than perhaps any where else, Edinburgh not exempted, as Ayrshire may witness, there having been more policy put down and trees planted than in any county of Scotland.

18 Oct 1817 Hepburn, Nursery man K—says he knew him well, he was a man of rough manners but of a heart fraught with the milk of human kindness. he was told of such a neighbour who prayed regularly—Well says he "I pray none & my Corn grows as well as his"

His sons are Thomas nursery & seed man Kilmarnock

William Merchant   do

John

When Tam son John was thought dying at Ochiltree—Rev Mr. Grant visited him—& thinking him an infidel said he would return & hoped to awaken his conscience. Awaken my conscience exclaimed John, you may as well fire a cannon at a dead man's arse as think to awaken my conscience.

Wm Tannahill, Ardrossan[17]

Lambie, Thatcher, Stevenston Ayrshire says he led the Plough when Burns turned up on Lochlie the Mouse—it

[16] In October Grierson continued his tour of Ayrshire, visiting Kilmarnock, Stevenston, and Ardrossan. See also note 12 above.

[17] Grierson here notes the name of someone to call on later.

had an uncommonly large nest. Next day while he was composing the Poem on the mouse, he was driving & unloading two [two (deleted)] carts, earth & lime, which his brother & and (sic) another man filled from a heap at a distance—so absorbed was he Burns that one time he forgot to unload one of the Carts and returned it with its load to the heap, not much to the pleasure of his Brother.

Burns was an excellt Plow & workman but when under the Influence of the Poetic fever [fervour?], not steady—then he was silent with his lips frequently in motion. So good natured that his boys directed him rather than he the boys. That night he 'brought the Partrick to the ground'[18] he told Lambie he was going to see his lass and L followed him to Betty Patons on a neighbour farm.

When residing at Lochlea——————————Agnes Brown, his mother, had been to visit a child that was dying in the neighbourhood—when she returned she said to her son Rab you should have been there—you never heard such a prayer as James Lee gave beside the poor child—he replied oh mother! Can you or Jamie Lee be so daft as to think that his prayer can be of any service to the dying Bairn or keep the devil at a distance or that God would send a child to the world to Damn it. On this his mother lifted the tongs to strike him with but he made his escape

Tanahill joiner Ardrossan when a little boy, was employed by Rot. Bowie after mercht Kilmarnock to go to Mossgiel & desire Bell Burns to go out to speak to him. This he had

---

[18] "Epistle to Rankine," H&H I, 178. Lambie's recollections do not coincide with the facts. Burns himself dates the turning up of the mouse as November, 1785, when he was living at Mossgiel. Betty Paton's child was born May 22, 1785, and was therefore conceived in 1784 when Burns was living at Mossgiel. Just when he began to visit her is uncertain, but it was probably while she was a servant at Lochlie, from which the Burnses moved in the spring of 1784. Lambie's assigning a particular night is either naïve or presumptuous.

done repeatedly, & stoped (*sic*) some times a while in the kitchen till Bell returned. he would not tell his name but said he came from Stewarton—once he met her mother at the door who cried into the house, 'Bell here's the Stewarton boy wanting you again—what the plague can he be ay wanting with you—his Breeches would not be mittens to a plowman. She had been a woman of some humor. he was some times sitting near to Bowie & Bell and when anything droll occurred in conversation—Bell would very readily turn it into meter—Bowie had not succeeded in his courtship of her & never married.

E. Memorandum on Highland Mary.[19]

1817 24 Oct   Met with   Campbell spouse to James Anderson mason in Ardrossan 1817 and sister to Highland Mary Burns friend.   She says Mary was tall, fair haird with blue eyes—they were daughters of Arch. Campbell mariner who resided at Dunoon Parish & Agnes Campbell his spouse, he died in Greenock 1815 & is buried in a lair of the new buring (*sic*) ground he bought from widow McPherson & his widow lives there in Scots land long vennal. Their sons are Robert & Archd Carpenters there—Mrs Andersons sons possess the Bible Burns gave her in exchange—it is printed by Alexander Kincaids assignies (*sic*) at Edin 1782.   The book sellers mark 5/6 2 vol small 12° on each vol is his mason mark.[20] this son a mason works presently in Paisley.   Mrs. A says her sister was buried in the old kirk ground Greenock, the new burying ground was not then begun & that widow McPherson & others

---

[19] See my "Burns' Highland Mary," *PMLA*, LII, 3; also Train MS, *post*.

[20] Given in the margin thus:

know the place—during the fever she was insensible.[21]
Mrs. A showed the Bible to J. G. which she sent to Paisley
to her son for, on purpose—on the first vol is in Burns hand
writing 'And ye shall not swear by my name falsely'—'I am
the LORD' 'Levit 19 Chap 12 verse' his name had been
there but carefully rubed (sic) out except some letters

On the second vol there is also wrote in his hand 'Thou
shalt not for swear thy self but shalt perform unto the
Lord thine Oath' 'Matth: 35 Ch 33 verse On this vol had
also been the mason mark & his name with date 1786.
but papers had been pasted on & torn off so the writing
is much defaced.

Leaves are folded in at or near various places as Isaiah
30 & 21. 34 & 10. 43 & 17. 55 & 16 [or 17 or 19] Jerem: x27.[22]
31 & 5. Ezek 18. 36 & 33. Hosea 4th 11 & 8. Zach. 13 Luke
17 & 14 John 13 & 14. 20 & 7. Rev 4 & 10

It seems evident that those two texts wrote at length in
his hand, each *only* part of a verse & inscribed one in each
vol. given to mary were intended strongly to alude (sic)
to some secret known to them alone & it is more than
probable this was some promise or Oaths he has not Oaths
as in the original but *Oath* & he was not one of these men
who had no meaning for what they did.—probably it was
her who erased the name, conscious too of the meaning and
not chusing to have the books in her possession on which
were the texts connected with the name.[23]

[21] Grierson's marginal note: "Except the last day of her life when
her father asked if she knew where she was. Yes, she said, I am on
my bridal bed. She died in the house of her uncle Alex Campbell,
Greenock Her grandfather was tenant to Duke of Argyle but lost
his farm rather than let his sons go into the army."

[22] Doubtful; it may be x & 7; or possibly simply Jerem 7; and
perhaps Jerem 1 & 7.

[23] While too much should not be made of the passages marked in
Mary's Bible, "Isaiah 30 & 21. 34 & 10." repeats the theme of the quo-

F. Further Notes[24] on Highland Mary

The mason mark of Robert Burns from the Pocket Bible, 1 vol exchanged with Mary Campbell ◁–✕–◁
Highland Mary from Dunoon Parish Cowal   The following words are from the same vol: "And ye shall not swear by my name falsely—I am the Lord Lev 19th Chap 12 verse

Robert Burns, Mossgiel had been wrote with his own hand on another blank leaf, but is carefully rubbed out except some letters
On the second vol

Thou shall not forswear thyself but perform unto the Lord thine oath
Matth 5 ch 33 verse

G. A letter addressed to "James Grierson Esqr of Dalgoner," in John Richmond's hand, and signed by him,

---

tations from Leviticus and Matthew inscribed on the flyleaves of the Bible, "Jerem 31 & 5" possibly refers to Burns' plan for taking Mary with him to the West Indies, and "Ezek 18" suggests repentance and forgiveness. "Hosea 4th 11 & 8.," "Zach. 13.," "Luke 17 & 14.," and "Rev 4 & 10" have a marked flavor of the Armour episode and its aftermath. In "John 13 and 14" there may be a reference to the famous ceremony of parting between Burns and Mary. Perhaps the greatest interest and puzzle of these references is their preservation by Mary's family.

[24] Written on a sheet containing a copy in Grierson's hand of "Rob Rhymer's earnest cry and Prayer to the Right Honble & Honble the Scotch Representatives in the House of Commons 1785-6." Except in one line, Grierson's text differs only in minor details of spelling and punctuation from the text of H&H based on two MSS and the Kilmarnock edition. The important variant is in line 4, stanza xxvii; Grierson reads "Their fields & groves" instead of "The scented groves." The poem is docketed, "Copied by Mr. John Richmond writer from Alex Carfrae Printer Anchor Close 22 August 1817." This may be the source of the clue Grierson followed in seeking out Mrs. Anderson, whom he saw two days later.

giving the circumstances surrounding the composition of "To a Haggis."

Sir:

As you expressed a wish to know the occasion that gave rise to Burns poem on the Haggis, It was the following as nearly as I can remember.

A party of Friends annualy (*sic*) for some years met at the House of David Shaw in Craigie Kirkdyke in the end of Harvest, and a sheeps haggis being presented it was called the Haggis Club.

At the meeting 1785 were present

Matthew Dickie writer in Edinburgh
William Paterson writer Kilmarnock
William Brown writer there
James Neil writer Ayr, of Shaws or Barnweil
Alexander Walker writer Edinr
Robert Burns &c

About eight days previous to the meeting A. Walker engaged Burns to meet him alone at Craigie Kirkdyke, where they should dine upon a Haggis—The novilty (*sic*) of Dining on a Haggis was much the Conversation at the engagement and on the Munday (*sic*) following He told me he had prepared an adress (*sic*) to the Haggis, On the Saturday following I accompanied Burns to Craigie Kirkdyke And was much surprised at meeting with so large a company,—At Dinner it was hinted to Matt Dickie the preses to ask Burns to Say the Grace. He rose up, and prefaced by saying He would address the (*sic*) by the Lord. And repeated the Address to the Haggis, there was no laughing in the Company every one thought that it was composed Extempore but the Poet told them, He came prepared for the Haggis but not for the Company, It was a Hearty Jovial meeting I am your

Humbl Svt

John Richmond

Writer

Mauchline 17 Decr 1817

H. Transcript, in Grierson's hand, of a letter[25] from Burns to John Richmond.

My dear Richmond

I am all impatience to hear of your fate, since the old confounder of right & wrong has turned you out of place by his journey to answer his indictment at the Bar of the other world.—He will find the Practice of that Court so different from the Practice in which he has for so many years been thoroughly hackney'd, that his friends, if he had any connection truly of that kind, which I rather doubt, may well tremble for his Sake.—

His Chicane, his left handed Wisdom, which stood so firmly by him to such good purpose *here,* like other accomplices in robbery and plunder, will, now the piratical business is blown, in all probability turn King's evidence, and then—The Devil's bag piper will touch him of "Bundle and go" X If he has left you any Legacy, I beg your pardon for all this, if not, I know you will swear to every word I have said about him.

I have lately been rambling over by Dunbarton & Inverary; and running a drunken race on the side of Loch

[25] Ferguson *119,* I, 100. This transcript was certainly secured from Richmond himself and it is, therefore, the best authority for the text of this letter, since neither the original nor a draft is now known. A collation with the published text reveals one important variant; the phrase "let me know of course" is given in Grierson's MS as "let me know by Connel," a preferable reading. Connel was the carrier between Mauchline and Edinburgh.

Lomond with a wild Highland man, his horse which had never known the ornaments of iron or leather zigzagged across before my old spavin'd hunter whose name is Jenny Geddes, and down came the Highland man horse & all, and down came Jenny and my Bardship; so I have got such a Skinful of bruises & wounds that I shall at least be four weeks before I dare venture on my Journey to Edinburgh.—

Not one new thing under the sun has happened in Mauchline since you left it.—I hope this will find you as comfortably situated as formerly, or, if Heaven please, more so; but, at all events, I trust you will let me know by Connel how matters stand with you, well or ill.

Tis but poor consolation to tell the world when matters go wrong; but, you know very well your connection & mine stands on a very different footing.—

I am ever

my dear friend

yours

Robt Burns

Mossgiel 7 July
    1787

X William Wilson W S died June 1787 aged 98. He had that morning wrote a suspension with his own hand which J. Richmond presented next day to Lord Braxfield who said what hocus pocus is this. I had a note this morning of his death. [Grierson's note]

I. Notes[26] on William Creech

I have settled matters greatly to my satisfaction with Mr. Creech—he is certainly not what he should be, nor has he given me what

[26] On a mere scrap; one side contains the first item, a tracing headed "Facsimile Burns," from a letter, Ferguson, *315*, I, 308, from Burns to his wife; below it is the anecdote, and on the reverse side the note of explanation.

A person met Burns coming up Leith walk brandishing a sapling & with much violence in his face & manner, said, Burns what is the matter? I am going to smash that S Creech.

FacSimile of Part of a letter Burns to his wife & given by her to her sister in law Mrs Adam Armour, Machline. Mr Creech—Bookseller, and afterwards Lord Provost of Edinburgh subscribed for 500 copies of the edition of 1787 which Burns went to Edinr to print instead of going to Jamaica. Creech on delivery refused to give more than the Booksellers price wh Burns thought taking the advantage of him after subscribing without restriction.

Notes of 1829-1830

Grierson left no important records after 1817 until these[27] of the years 1829-1830.

A. Memorandum of a conversation with Clarinda, 1829.

14-12-29

Called on Mrs. McLehose a well looked little woman, plump, is 70 next birthday was married at 17. had 4 children one son only alive a W S. born in five years when her husband went to Kingston Jamaica. She went there Feb 1792 and stoped (*sic*) only 3 months the heat was so excessive & mosquitos so anoying (*sic*).

Burns was last in Edin Dec. 1791 and no more that she knew of—Jan End of 1787[28] that she was acquainted with him

[27] Item A occupies a single sheet, and item B another; item C shares a scrap with the name of a butcher, the price of beef, train schedules and fares, wages paid to gleaners, etc.
[28] Really 1788.

Her husband died 1812

Burns told her that his fame would be greater after death than in life.

She was much surprised that Burns should should (*sic*) designate his wife bonny who was so grime—told her that Mrs B' brother Adam said that it was not his sister he called bonny Jean but Jane Lorimer of Kemys hall near Ellisland. She was Chloris & the lassie with the lint white locks.

She was born 1760 married 1777

The way the letters came to be published—a young man Finley, a literary person who died in early life at or near Lanark, asked for them to excerpt some parts into an acct. of Burns. those parts she marked when to her great surprise the whole was published.

Mrs. Gray formerly of Edin.[29] & after Belfast accademy (*sic*) who died some years ago at Bombay, the last thing she had in hand was a vindication of Mrs. McLehose from aspersions or suspicions with respect to Burns" (*sic*).

She went to Kingston Jamaica to her husband Feb 1792 & stoped (*sic*) scarce 3 months she was so much anoyed (*sic*) with muiskitos & the Climate[30] Burns in marrying Jean Armour behaved better than Jean could have expected—but B said in the situation she was and hurried out of doors by her father what could he do. Mrs Mac does not approve of the Posthumous monuments—they are idle & farsical (*sic*).

15 Dec.

Went to see the Jolly Beggars which Greenshields has embodied so admirably in stone, to be packed up for Edinr next day. Wrote to Clarinda to see them—[three words

[29] Burns' correspondent, Mary Peacock.

[30] To say nothing of her husband's ebony mistress and mahogany children.

illegible]. On passing from Lanark to Nethan waterfoot
met many people returning from viewing this Groupe (*sic*)
traveling by every sort of conveyance a Coach, Gigs, many
Carts & horsemen & Multitudes on foot. Not less perhaps
than a thousand per day from the various quarters and
this for many days

Jany 1831 Statue of Burns, after Taylor, exhibiting in
    Edinr.—by Greenshields.

  B. Memorandum of a Conversation with Clarinda, 1830.

    Where e'er we go, whatever realms we see
    Our heart untraveled, fondly turns to thee England
      Goldsmith
                    Page 2 Col 9 London Weekly Times
                        4 Nov 30

    Whatever place, whatever land I see,
      My heart untravell'd fondly turns to Thee,
    Still to Clarinda turns—with Ceaseless pain,
      And drags at each remove, a lengthened chain[31]

---

[31] These lines not in Grierson's hand. The following notes (on a
sheet with "Burns grace at Kirkudbright" and the anecdote of Jamie
Todd (see *post*), and a debased version of "O, Wert Thou in the
Cauld Blast") and draft of a letter (on a separate sheet) resulted from
this interview with Clarinda:
                        From Glasgow Herald of 12 Nov 30
Burns looked into a room where some persons was enjoying them-
selves & was retiring when one of them called, come in Johnny Bopeep.
After it was proposed that he who wrote the best verse should be
kept free when Burns wrote
                Here I am Johnny Bopeep
                I saw three sheep
                And those three sheep saw me
                Half a crown apiece
                Will pay for their fleece
                And so Johnny Bopeep gets free
In the Dfrs Journal of 9 nov 30 It is said these lines were from
Drummond and that Burns would not have borrowed them, but they
did not know Burns who said so.

The above is part of a letter[32] subscribed, Sylvander, Burns, to Clarinda, Mrs. McLehose, 1789, copied out for J. G. 24 Nov. 30 & partly read to him at same time by Clarinda.

Inter alia of much in the same style writes I have been to see a certain person, Jean Armour, but oh how insipid and disgusting compared to you.

When Clarinda heard of the marriage she was much shocked it was so utterly unexpected by her and so much at variance with what had passed—but for that she had

---

Drummond's lines on a similar occassion (*sic*) were

    I bopeep
    Saw your four sheep
    And each of you his fleece
    The reckning is five shilling
    If each of you is willing
    Tis fifteen pence a piece

Goldsmith in Italy says of his country—
    Where eer we go, whatever realms we see
    Our hearts, untravel'd, fondly turn to thee.

Burns
    Whatever plain, whatever land I see
    My heart, untraveled, fondly turns to thee,
    Still to Clarinda turns with ceaseless pain
    And drags at each remove, a lengthened chain

B does not seem quite at home when he borrows note the difference between the first two lines & the two last. Something like the following might apply to Clarinda.
    What ever face, what ever shapes I see,
    Improv'd in mind or dress as they may be
    My heart unwitched fondly turns to thee
    Still to Clarinda turns, with ceaseless pain
    And drags at each remove a lengthening chain.

Mr. Editor

In your journal of Nov a correspondent censures the credulity of the Scotsman for admiting (*sic*) that Burns parodied the Johnny Bopeep of Drummund tho it is strictly in character with him in a time of Jolity (*sic*) and tho' perhaps no one wit borrowed less, who

not gone to the West Indies. She says 1790 Burns offered her a visit, which she declined as he was married.[33]

Also, For as unkindly as Jeans father had behaved to Burns, that when he returned from Edinr with his pockets full he was received very graciously and Jean & him locked into a room

Miss Nimmo—a friend of Peggy Chalmers Mrs————[34] introduced Clarinda to Burns.

C. Dinner with Robert Ainslie and A. C. McLehose, W. S.

Burns, a stranger, was invited into a seat at Church by a Lady. The text was the Terrors of the Gospel denouncing all sinners to hell the lady seemed attentive but agitated he wrote in the blank leaf of the bible wt a pencil

> Fair maid, you need not take the hint,
> Nor idle texts pursue
> Twas only sinners that he meant
> Not angels such as you

———

wrote so much yet I have an other in my eye from a letter 1791 not printed and which it is likely never will be printed the one version is:

> Whatever plain, whatever land I see
> My heart untraveled fondly turns to theeX

Goldsmith in Italy says of England

> Where eer I go, whatever realms I see
> My heart untravel'd fondly turns to the

X Still to   turns, with ceaseless pain
  and drags at each remove a lengthened chain
  28 Dec '30

absence prevented this being sent sooner. If the above is printed please throw of (sic) six casts which will be called & paid for.

[32] Ferguson, 210, I, 194.

[33] Cp. Ferguson, 388, 389, II, 8. Clarinda made no reference to the visit Burns paid her in 1791, just before her departure for Jamaica.

[34] Mrs. Lewis Hay; properly identified in Train MS.

Mr. Ainslie who accompanied Burns to Kelso told J. G. while dining with A C McLehose WS that his sister was the person these lines were addressed to.[35]

Notes on Second Election Ballad

In the notes below, Grierson used his knowledge of local affairs to illustrate Burns' second election ballad.[36]

"Notes to Burns election song Stewartry of Kirkcud 1795

Mar 1816"

Verse 1. Murray of Broughton[37]

Rev. Wm Nesbit Firth Parish, for adultery, imprisoned fed on bread & water 2 mos & banished

2. Muray (sic) p 5. 20

2. Gordon of Balmaighie—Grace Johnston of Carnsalloch mistress to Murray was niece to Gordon, his sister's daughter, & mother to the present Murrays—see notes to trogging by Burns[38] Wm Bushby went to India 1776 returned 1786 died at Tinwald Downs 16 Aug 1813 In great horror[39] it was said—conj Miss Griz Maitland 1776.

3. John Bushby, writer & sheriff clerk in Dumfries who succeeded the office [one word illegible] for £800

James Dickson Sh. Clerk who died Ap 1776 John was Bankrupt 1797 for £80,000 chiefly to the Douglas & Heron Bank which commenced 1769 & was Bankrupt in two years to the loss of more than £2000 each share to

[35] Cp. H&H II, 433.

[36] H&H, II, 193 & 403-5. Cp. Young MS and Hope MS, post.

[37] Grierson here compares the punishment of a poor clergyman with the immunity of a great man who had committed the same offense.

[38] The "notes to trogging," that is to Burns' ballad "The Trogger," are not among the present papers.

[39] Cp. Train MS, post.

those who were able to stand. See Scots Mag 1789 p 204 Ẋ

Ẋ John M'Adam of C he opened a bank at Ayr 17 Octr 1763 who resigned in favour of Doug Heron & Co bank 1769 as did the bank at Dfs. DH&Co annuities redeemed 1774-106-1967 Scots Mag. 1763-581 do 1773—668. Ayr Bank discontinued from 12 Aug 1773.

X John first married miss Newall of Barskeoch 2 Miss Maitland of Eccles

4. Kempleton's Birkie Wm youngest Brother to John Bushby, who got him in oposition (*sic*) to great intrest (*sic*) from Lord North & who applied for relations a writer's place in the East India company's Service & he returned in ten years with a large fortune, supposed by some uncharitable people, to have been partly Spoils from the ruin of that Bank, of which John was Director & chief agent. his brother in law John McVitie teller for Dumfries and his brother Thomas Bushby of Ard [several letters illegible] & after collector of the customs at Kirkcudbt had the Contract for furnishing the bank with Gold & Silver.

5. John, son to sd John Bushby had lately been appointed sheriff of Wigton Sh and his brother Sheriff Clerk of Dumfries a Short time before his fathers death. he obtained the Estate of Eccles after the death of his uncle Cap John Maitland. After a very singular oposition (*sic*) from his aunts Miss maitland and Mrs D— [Dr?] Babbington of the episcopal chapel Dfs the heirs at Law

6. Some read Maxwell of Cardoness others Gordon of Carleton

7. New Christening towns—Newton Stewart they got created a Burgh by the Name of Newton Douglass—& Castle

Douglass was formerly named Carlingwark & Caswayind. Sir Wm Douglass who died 22 Sep 1809 traveled through Galloway a chapman he once was swindled out of a knife on the road there—a Gentleman came past while he was weeping & gave him half a crown. this he told. It was alledged (sic) they insured vessels to america & laid plans for their being taken. It was thought the Douglasses, so rich, were fond of paying their respects to Lord Galloway.

When John Anderson of Finnary [?] bought the Estate of Lord Barrymore Sir Wm was the only man he could find able to advance the money to him.

7 8 Gordon of Kenmure Kenmure was elected 1778 when the election was set aside for bribery practiced by David Newal writer Dfr. A duel took place that election betwixt Gordon of Kenmure and Spalding of Holm who promised his vote but resiled on being offered a writership for his Brother in India—was wounded in the side.

Once same Spalding Brought drunk out of Balmaghie boat & laid cross an horse before his servant & so carried to Crossmichael village.

8 June 1801 he died at Dainvile park a house he built

9. Cap Walter Laurie of Red Castle, explanatory enough—his Grandfather's tittle (sic) was Clautenpluck—he changed the name of the place to Laurieston—but some continued in scorn to call him Clautenpluck—he would have answered De'il pluck the saul out of ye.

—he was a very little man—a land lady once made a bill reckoning one short of the number in company—she was called in & desired to reckon again which she did making the number as before, when it was observed to her as was noticed,—she had missed Mr. Laurie, pointing to him—

O says she 'as for little master' clasping his hand, 'I do not mind him'—Mr L was 45 but sat with his back to the Land lady

10 Lord Gorlies

11 Rev James Muirhead minister of the Parish of Urr—Maxwell minister of the Parish of Buitle

12 Earl Selkirk

13 Oswald of Auchencruive

14 Nabobs The Hannays Sir Sam M P for Camelford died 1792

Mr Wm Copland of Collieston & Mollins remarkable for large whiskers—

he married Helen daug of Sir James Dunbar of Mochrum 6 Jany 1773 ob 6 Aug 1808

2. McAdam of Craigengillan after living with Miss Walker from 1798 he one day 22 Mar 1805 called in his servants & acknowledged a marriage with her & shot himself instantly. After a teugh (sic) lawsuit the house of Peers declared the marriage legal & her ⨍ (sic) sons & [or 2] daugh his heirs

Four Additional Items

There remain to be mentioned four miscellaneous items.

1. Twenty-two notes scattered through the papers (extending from 1803 to 1834, many copied or clipped from newspapers) chiefly concerning various monuments to Burns, deaths of members of his family, and the erection of the Dumfries mausoleum. They have no importance and have not been reproduced.

2. A broadside, "HALLOWEEN by R. Burns," one side of a sheet 8 x 11 in., printed in three columns, a condensed

version beginning with H&H stanza VII and omitting stanzas IX, X, XI, XII, XV, XVI, and XXVIII. Not collated. It bears this docket, "22 Augt 1817 Received from Mr. Carfrae, Printer, son of Mrs. Carfrae Upper Baxter's Close Edinr with whom Richmond & Burns lodged."

3. An "improbable," "Burns grace at Kirkudbright"

> Some have meat & cannot eat
> Some can not eat that want it
> But we have meat & we can eat
> Sae let the Lord be thankit.

4. An anecdote, without authority, dated November, 1830.

Burns in a churchyard in Glenkens, Galloway, made the grave diger (*sic*) Jamie Todd drunk & pulled him behind a through Stone. When the funeral came, they found the grave half done & James absent, they imagined he had been buried alive and set to work to relieve him.—Some of the mourners wandering about found in chalk on a grave stone the following explanation

> Under this stone lies Jamie Todd
> He is not dead but drunk by God

III

THE TRAIN MANUSCRIPT

III

THE TRAIN MANUSCRIPT

Richmond previous to Burns' residence with him paid 2/6
p Week for Room-rent—[then *(deleted)*] the[ir *(deleted)*]
rent was increased to 3/— when Burns came to live with
him—(a Mrs Carfrae the landlady)

Davie Sillar still lives and is, or was lately, chief magistrat
(sic) (of Machline—I think) By the death of an uncle a
partner in a mercantile house in Liverpool of the firm
of Sillar & Henderson, he succeeded to a fortune of
£30,000, or £40,000.

"Corn rigs" [were bonny o' *(deleted)*] This song was written
in compliment to Annie Rankine—now Mrs Merry.—
Mr Grierson asked Mrs Merry if she remembered the
particular night referred to among "the barley."—She
said, *No,* with considerable näiveté, *(sic)* but added: "I
mind o' mony a happy night wi him, tho'" She was
daughter to "rude rough ready witted Rankine"—Rankine died 2d Feby 1810 and is buried in Galston Churchyard.

Connected with the State of his health mentioned at page
20 of Mr Lockharts Life, Mr Grierson was informed by
one who was his [Burns'] bedfellow, (but whose name I

forget), previous to his leaving Ayrshire that even at that early period these nocturnal faintings and suffocations were so frequent he always kept a large tub filled with cold water in the place where he slept, and often during the night he rose and plunged himself among the cold water which gave instant relief.—

In page 23. "the sweet sonsie lass" alluded to had afterwards a child to Burns.—Her name was Bettey Paton.[1]

Holy Willie.—This worthy met with the death of "poor Maillie." He had fallen into most dissipated habits—and was found dead one morning in a ditch, into which he had fallen while drunk.

Highland Mary.—Truth deprives her history of much of its charm.—Her character was loose in the extreme.—She was *kept* for some time by a Brother of Lord Eglinton's, and even while a servant with Gavin Hamilton, [two words, "her at" (?), deleted] and during the period of Burns' attachment it was well known that her meetings with Montgomery were open and frequent.—The friends of Burns represented to him the impropriety of his devotedness to her, but without producing any change in his sentiments.—Richmond told Mr Grierson that Montgomery & Highland Mary frequently met [one word, "at" (?), deleted] in a small alehouse called the Elbow—and upon one occasion he & some of Burns's friends knowing they were actually together in the Elbow—and having often in vain tried to convince Robert of her infidelity, upon this occasion they promised to give ocular proof of their assertions.—The party retired to the Elbow—Richmond (Mr Grierson's informant) was one and they took their seats in the kitchin (*sic*) from which

---

[1] Here Train is in error. She was Nelly Kirkpatrick, whose relations with Burns were innocent.

two rooms branched off to the right and left—being all the accommodation the house contained.—They had taken their position in the kitchin *(sic)*, to be sure that no one could leave the [house *(deleted)*] other rooms without being observed.—After waiting long, and when Burns was beginning to ridicule their suspicions, at last Mary Campbell appeared from one of the rooms—was jeered by the party, in a general way—blushed and re- tired.—Another long interval elapsed and Burns began to rally his spirits, which were very much sunk—and [one word, "at" (?), deleted] Montgomery (Colonel or Capt) walked out of the same room.—Burns coloured deeply—compressed his lip—and muttered, "*damn* it." After enduring considerable bantering from his friends he soon gave way to the general hilarity of the evening, and his friends thought he had seen enough of Highland Mary but in a few days after, he returned "like the dog to its vomit."

Clarinda—Richmond informed Mr Grierson that one day this personage called at their lodgings for Burns who had gone out.—Richmond knew her well, and also the nature of the intimacy which existed between her and the Poet—and he instantly volunteered his services to find out Burns—but so affraid *(sic)* were both he and Clarinda (Mrs Maclehose) that she should be discovered he locked her into their appartment *(sic)* & took the key with him.—Being unsuccessful in his search to find Burns, he at last returned and liberated the Prisoner.[2]—

Of Clarinda, Mr Grierson gives the following account— I cannot say on what authority.—Her husband had been unsuccessful in mercantile speculations, and *retired* to the West Indies.—Sometime afterwards Clarinda fol-

[2] See my "Burns' Highland Mary," *PMLA*, LII, 3.

lowed, and after a tedious [passage *(deleted)*] voyage when the vessel neared the coast of the island where her husband resided and was compelled to wait an increase of tide, so impatient was the lady to fly on the wings of love to her lord that during the night she put in to land in the Ships boat—and through the gloom of midnight approached the house where she expected to enjoy the delight of an [a few letters deleted] unexpected meeting after a long separation.—She entered—was ushered into some room—or ushered herself—where she should meet him, and to her astonishment and horror she found him fast asleep in the arms of a sable beauty!—She uttered not one word—walked out of the room—retraced her steps to the vessel—again took possession of her Cabin and in due time returned to Scotland without ever again setting foot on shore, or seeing her husband.

Mr Grierson has been informed that a quantity of letters *from* Clarinda *to* Burns, are still in existence—that these letters fell into the hand of some one who threatened their publication—but at last, on conditions that her own letters should be returned to her, she gave up the Poet's, as they afterwards appeared.—A transcript was said to have been taken from her letters which [one or more words deleted] *may* one day appear. (Mr Rob Chambers once met with Clarinda, and heard her relate some particulars of an interview she once had with Godwin, when Godwin was absurdly taciturn.) —

Epitaph on Wee Johnnie—although this epitaph appears in the first Kilmarnock Edition of Burns' Poems, Mr Grierson says in Ayrshire it is quite well known that the Wee Johnnie was John Wilson his Printer.

Creech—Some mysterious circumstances connected with the quarrel between Burns and this publisher are as yet undivulged.—Report, which *I* have often heard, says that Creech was supposed to have smuggled an Edition into the Market unknown to Burns. It is said that Creech sent to Beugo for the Portrait (copper)—that Beugo thought it odd that Creech should do so, and assured of the Bookseller's keenness, he put a private mark upon the plate Report addeth that numberless copies of the Poems afterwards appeared with this private mark upon the portrait. Mr Grierson shewed me a fragment of a letter from Burns to his wife—which the latter gave to him—as she had done the remainder of the letter to sundry collectors of relics, which fragment runs thus:— "I have settled with Creech, very much to my satisfaction, but he is not"—This is ambiguous enough in all conscience. Mr Grierson says the misunderstanding between Burns and Creech was accomplished by the interference of a mutual friend a Mrs Hay—wife of Mr Lewis Hay Banker in Edinr.—He thinks she or her husband are still alive, and that they are possessed both of abundant materials and recollections regarding the History of Burns.—

Highland Mary.—I should have added formerly that Grierson has a facsimile of the leaf of the Bible *exchanged* by Burns with Mary containing the inscription.—in addition to what has already appeared in print the Signature of Burns is followed by his Mason's Mark which if you are a *free* mason you will understand—It is thus: >—×—▷ In place of any of the commonplace facsimiles generally given of Burns' handwriting, it is likely we will give a representation of the two leaves containing these inscriptions. Mr Grierson was permitted by the surviving relations to copy these inscriptions.—One curious circumstance is worth recording.—From what motive it is now difficult to say, but one of Mary Campbell's brothers pasted a slip of paper over the *signatures* of Burns—and to read these it is necessary to hold the [light *(deleted)*] leaf between the eye and the light.—I saw a letter from another of her brother's *(sic)* to Mr Grierson stating this circumstance—and containing a lock of Mary's hair.— (It is of the true Celtic hue, and *feel*) This contains some other interesting information.—I am promised copies of it—and of several other unpublished letters of Burns, by Mr G.—These were read to me—but after some weeks exertion I have hitherto been unable to procure them.— Grierson is a curious old fellow.—He has been an enthusiastic collector of such matters connected with Burns for upwards of 20 years—during which time he has repeatedly visited the various places of the Poet's residences.—

Farm of Mossgiel—This farm taken by Gilbert & Rob Burns—was a *subset* from Gavin Hamilton, Writer, Machline.

The Armours.—Jean's' *(sic)* father was only a *working* mason

Burns Marriage—Jean Armour, and Rob Burns were privately married in the writing office of Gavin Hamilton, Machline, by John Farquhar Esq of [Gilsc *(deleted)*] Gilmillscroft, J. P.[3]

Twins—I presume you are aware that Jean brought forth Twins twice in 16 months—the first pair previous to marriage—and the latter very soon after.—On the birth of the

[3] It is possible that Train gave this information on his own authority. His father had been land steward on the Gilmilnscroft estate, which was formerly a part of Mauchline parish. Ch-W (II, 335) records three accounts of the marriage, including this one, but Train's intimate connection with Gilmilnscroft gives his version a distinct priority and makes it almost certain that at last the circumstances of Burns' final marriage to Jean Armour have been established.

first twins Burns was at the plough and Jeans brother
Adam Armour was sent to inform him.—Burns came to
her that evening with a guinea, and some Tea and Sugar,
"which" (says Mr Grierson, my informant) was thought
handsome"

Mrs. Dunlop—She was daughter to Sir Thomas Wallace of
Craigie

The Learned Pig.—After some stay in Edinr Burns was
much *taken out,* and he was honoured with many invita-
tions, some of which appeared to him quite uncalled
for.—In short he saw that he was looked upon by numbers as one of the *Lions* of the day, and upon being
very much pressed to join some company he, at last,
observed "On one condition I shall come It is that you
secure the Learned Pig also to be of the Party."—The
Learned Pig was exhibiting in Edinr, at the time.—

Mr Murdoch—It is difficult to put a nursery story in en-
durable language—but Mr Grierson mentioned a juvenile
anecdote of Burns which serves to illustrate your observa-
tions at the top of page 14.—While a mere child, and at
Mr M's school some person called one day on the
Teacher, who went out for a few minutes.—As is quite
customary in village schools a dreadful uproar commenced.—Mr Murdoch, at last returned—and in the
meantime Robert whose seat was near the door had
slipped into a press quite contiguous to it.—To quell
the uproar Mr M struck the *tawz* loudly against the press-
door.—Rob was behind it and screamed out and began
to cry so loudly that he was at last suffered to go home.—
His mother questioned what was the matter.—Robert
could not answer for sometime—but by and by sobbed
out "the-mas-master *payed* me! *Payed* you Robbie what
for did the master pay ye?—Where did he pay you on?—

He pay—payed me on the press!" added poor Robert
which created much amusement to his mother—and was
long a standing joke at his expense.—

Unpublished Letters & Poems.—Of the former Mr Grierson
has several given him by Richmond and others.—He read
me one on the death of Richmond's master a very worthy
and very aged writer—Another which refers to the situation of Jean—in which he jocularly alludes to his smug-
gling propensities and says since the cargoes come double
he has some thoughts of commencing free Trader.—
Another written under terrible excitation of feeling,
when he was skulking from the misery of a jail.—Mr G.
has also some Poems.—One an Epitaph on a Miss Burns—
a certain frail sister who had availed herself of his popu-
larity to adopt his name.—Another quite in his master-
vein in the style of Holy Willie's prayer.—It is a sort
of pennance for having assisted to ride the stang on
Racer Jess who being a favourite with one of the Eglin-
toun family soon had a party of military sent to her
assistance.—There is a long poem also in existance (*sic*)
intitled (*sic*) The Poet's Rambles on the Banks of the
Ayr." It is said to be his longest production—Richmond
has, or had it.—He goes up the one side of the River, and
down the other satyrizing in his most unrelenting manner
if (*sic*) [one word, "gentl" (?), deleted] family situated
upon the adjoining country.—It can never be printed—
neither can any of the others alluded to above—at least
entire.[4]—

[4] Of these items and the letter from Highland Mary's brother mentioned previously, only the epitaph on Miss Burns and the letter
on the death of Richmond's employer are now among the papers.
The other two letters are obviously Ferguson *240*, I, 221; and *37*, I,
35. The poem on Racer Jess is "Adam Armour's Prayer." Train's
note is the only known reference to "The Poet's Rambles on the
Banks of the Ayr."

IV

THE YOUNG MANUSCRIPT

IV

Memoir Regarding Robert Burns[1]

The first Life of Burns was written by my friend and Schoolfellow Dr. Currie of Liverpool. When he began the Work, I was on a visit to him and staid some days [with him *(deleted)*] at Liverpool, when we had [frequent some *(deleted)*] conversations respecting the Poet; I told the doctor that tho' I had a high admiration of his talents, [and regretted much that he had never been properly rewarded by the public, but yet at same time *(deleted)*] I thought he had brought [much *(deleted)*] a great part of his misfortunes upon himself by his own bad Conduct and propensity to Satire with very bad taste and little regard to truth, and [in particular, *(deleted)*] if he had [actually *(deleted)*] really possessed that [high proud *(deleted)*] proud spirit of freedom and independence to which he made loud claims, he never would have condescended to have become an *exciseman*. N L *(sic)* I found there were many points in the character of Burns which the Dr. did not admire, and I am possessed of letters from him which show that it was his purpose to gloss over his failings, and make the Book as

[1] Young's title. This note of explanation was apparently added after he had completed the memoir.

profitable as he possibly could for the benefit of the Bard's helpless family.

[It *(deleted)*] In this spirit it certainly was written and I humbly think that tho' many lives of Burns have since been published, Dr. Currie's and [beyond all comparison the best. Next to his *(deleted)*] after him, (if not superior to Dr Currie's) the best was Mr. Lockhart's, and perhaps there was room for *two* such works; but certainly the Ettrick Shepherd's, and some others which have since appeared, might well have been spared.—

After Dr. Currie's Life of Burns and Mr. Lockhart's publication, [which had likewise considerable merit, I think *(deleted)*] I should [not *(deleted)*] hardly have taken the trouble of perusing more of his Biography by other hands, but being accidentally in a reading room in a town in the South of England, a gentleman having taken up a volume of Allan Cunninghame's Life of Burns, and having exclaimed "that Poet seems to have had as many lives as a Cat," curiosity led me to peruse vol. III of [that *(deleted)*] the Work after the stranger had laid it down, and the [remarks and *(deleted)*] feelings & remarks excited by its perusal made me take some notes which at my first leisure I extended in reference to *"The 3d Volume of the Life and Works of Burns by Allan Cunninghame."*[2]—

Notes on perusal of Vol. III of
The Works of Burns by Allan
Cunningham.—

P. 201.[3] The Heron Ballads.

Mr. Cunningham does not give Mr. Heron his proper

---

[2] Allan Cunningham, *The Works of Robert Burns with His Life,* London, 1834. 8 vols.

[3] Really page 261. The error appears in the rought draft and is carried over into the fair copy.

designation.[4] It is true he had an estate in Galloway called *Kirrouchtree,* but his proper style was Patrick Heron of Heron, in the County of Lincoln; and a most amiable & excellent person he was, well entitled to represent in parlt. either the Stewartry or shire of Galloway, his native country;[5] but not likely to be aided in the attainment of that object by[6] the libels & lampoons of Burns, on all those who did not support, or were opposed to, Mr. Heron's political interests, with which Burns had no more to do than he had with the affairs of the man in the moon. But he[7] was pleased to spare me, and never even mentioned my name, in any of his abusive couplets or epigrams so plentifully circulated in Dumfriesshire and Galloway during these contested elections, altho' I may truly say *"quorum pass magna* &c.; for I was the [principal *(deleted)*] Lawagent [and conductor *(deleted)*] of in *(sic)* both these Contests, on the part of Mr. Gordon of Balmaghie and the Honble Montgomery Stewart.—

[Whence this happened *(deleted)*] Whence this forbearance originated, I [was *(deleted)*] am at a loss to account for, and can now only conjecture, from my recollection of the following circumstances.—

I was just entering into business when Burns came first to Edinburgh; and one of my first clients was his friend Wm. Nicol, one of the masters of the High School, who was the son of a Tailor in the village of Ecclefechan in Annandale, employed and patronized by my Grandfather and his family; which services were zealously returned to me

[4] Cunningham called Patrick Heron, "Heron of Kerroughtree."

[5] r.d. reads "county," corrected to "country."

[6] r.d. deletes, "such gratuitous blackguardism & folly as that which was practised and exhibited by Burns in his malignant."

[7] r.d. deletes, "re I cannot recollect without much satisfaction and even gratitude to Burns himself, that he spared me in all his lampoons."

by Mr. Nicol in the line of my profession. I considered him, and, I believe justly, as one of the greatest Latin Scholars [that ever existed *(deleted)*] of the Age; and when I found him & Burns over their Whiskey-punch, [(which I had some times[8] the honor of partaking with them) *(deleted)*] bandying *extempore* translations and imitations of English, Scotch & Latin Epigrams, I could not help considering them as good exemplifications of the Italian *Improvisatori*.

One remarkable instance still occurs to me. When Burns gave Nicol the following strange epitaph to translate into Latin,—

> "Here lies old John Hildibrode
> Have mercy on him, gude God,
> As he would hae on thee, if he were God
> And thou wert old John Hildibrode."

After a little consideration, Nicol gave furth *(sic)* a Latin edition of this nonsense; which I thought greatly superior to the original. I wrote it down, and long preserved it with some similar dogrel verses; but I now recollect the beginning only:—

> "Hic situs Hilbrodus,
> Quo non miserabilis alter" &c.

At this time, I looked upon Nicol as a far greater Poet and genius than Burns. He had considerable, indeed constant, employment in translating the Medical & Law Theses of the graduates at the University, for which he made liberal charges, but was very ill paid. I was employed by him to recover many of these claims [on *(deleted)*] from English students, concerning which I corresponded with the late Mr. Roscoe, (then an Attorney in Liverpool); and

---

[8] r.d. deletes, "frequently."

on communicating to Nicol some of Mr. Roscoe's letters signifying that several of his claims were considered to be doubtful, if not desperate, he fell into an extravagant rage, [and *(deleted)*] swore, the most unseemly oaths & uttered the grossest blasphemies, that "if our Saviour were again on Earth and had employed him to translate a Thesis without paying him for it, he would crucify him over again!" [From these *(deleted)*] In consequence of these and similar exhibitions, I thought it prudent to detach myself from [these *(deleted)*] such companions; but I never had any quarrel with them; and I believe I was chiefly indebted to this early [friendship *(deleted)*] this *(sic)* connection between Nicol & Burns for my *exemption* from the election pasquinades of [Burns *(deleted)*] the latter, [not that I was conscious that I had ever done anything to merit that favor, being at least as assailable as my clients Gordon of Balmaghie, Murray of Broughton, or Lord Galloway, &c.—⁹*(deleted)*]

During the whole election contest I had the good fortune to conduct matters in [the most *(deleted)*] a civil and cordial manner with Mr. Heron and his Agents, except on one occasion, when Mr. Heron took it into his head to write

⁹ r.d. version of this passage reads, "From these and similar exhibitions, I thought it prudent to detach myself [from such Companions *(deleted)*] from [my *(deleted)*] these Companions, [whom thereafter I most cautiously avoided, *(deleted)*] but I never had any quarrel with [them my companions *(deleted)*] them [& from that circumstance & some Kindness which I afterwards had it in my power to manifest towards Burns *(deleted)*] & I believe I was chiefly indebted to this Early friendship for my *exemption* from [his *(deleted)*] the Election Pasquinades [& Epigrams, *(deleted)*] of Burns not that I was conscious that I had ever done anything to merit [the distinction conferred by his malevolent abuses; Yet I was at *(deleted)*] that [public *(deleted)*] favour being at least as assailable as my Clients Balmaghie, Broughton, Lord Galloway &c [&c, who were certainly the most amiable and respectable characters in the whole district.—*(deleted)*]"

to me, that he had been credibly informed I had asserted that he and his lady (Lady Elizabeth Heron, sister to the Earl of Dundonald) had got a promise from Government, that, in the event of his being successful, they would get pensions [of nearly the amount *(deleted)*] of £1000., p ann and he required me, in terms, rather rude and peremptory, to name the persons on whose authority I had circulated such a scandalous falsehood.—

My answer to him was in the following words.

"Edinr 20 April 1801.[10]

"Altho' your request is not conveyed to me in the politest "terms, yet I have no hesitation to inform you that the "information you have received is destitute of truth. I "am content, Sir, with doing my duty for your antagonist "Mr. Stewart, without troubling myself about you or your "affairs, or descending to the meanness of inventing or "propagating a calumny to your prejudice.—

"If you have given any credit to the report of my being "the author of such a contemptible falsehood, I must take "the liberty of saying that you have paid no compliment "either to my character or your own penetration."—

On a subsequent meeting, Mr. Heron frankly told me he was convinced that I had had no hand in circulating the report which had induced him to write a hasty letter; and I assured him, I had never heard of it until I got that letter; and during the remainder of the contest—which ended, unhappily for him, in a committee of the House of Commons—we remained good friends. On taking leave

[10] Writing in 1834, nearly forty years after Burns' death, Young confuses the 1795 and 1796 elections for which Burns wrote the ballads, and a later one in 1802 when Mr. Heron was again successful but was unseated by a committee of the House of Commons, May 10, 1803. He died on June 9, at Grantham, on his way home to Scotland.

of him before he set out for Scotland when he was unseated, he said he had been ill used by others, but never by me.—

My uncle, Alexr. Orr of Waterside, was his Lawagent at the time I was bred to business in his office, and I had been very active and serviceable to Mr. Heron in prosecuting the divorce which he obtained against his first wife—a daughter of Lord Kames.—

A note of the Biographer's Mr A. Cunningham[11] bears, that Mr. Heron took his disappointment so much to heart, that he died *by his own hands,* [(as was believed) *(deleted)*] on his way back to Scotland. I never heard this before; and I think Mr. Heron was incapable of suicide. He was the successful candidate on the day of election at Kirkcudbt.; but, as agent for his antagonist, I presented a petition to the House of Commons against his return, and he was unseated by a committee. I saw him before and after their report to the House, and he seemed on both occasions to be in a bad state of health: I took leave of him [shortly before his departure for Scotland, not *(deleted)*] without any feelings of animosity.—[12]and I lamented his sudden death wh. I am convinced did not take place by his own hand—

Page 270.

In his third Election Ballad to the tune of "Buy broom besoms," Burns writes—

"Here's armorial bearings
    Frae the manse o'Urr;
The crest, a sour crab-apple,
    Rotten at the core.
        Buy braw troggin &c."

[11] Cunningham, III, 271-72.

[12] r.d. continues this sentence, "and yet I had more reason to be offended with him, than with [the conduct of *(deleted)*] his injudicious friend Mr. Robert Burns.—[towards me at least *(deleted)*]." But this addition is itself deleted.

The person here alluded to was Dr. James Muirhead, minister of the Gospel at Urr, who was a poet as well as Burns, an eminent scholar, and a man of considerable humour; many specimens of which I once had in my possession, but I can now bring to my recollection only some fragments.—

In the town of Dumfries, there lived an itinerant preacher,—who had been licensed, but never obtained a Kirk,— generally known by the name of *Professor Williamson*. He gained a scanty subsistence by going from house to house in Dumfriesshire and Galloway, acting as a pedagogue and an occasional preacher. In that capacity he had been employed in the family of James McWhirter, a Bleacher & Stocking-weaver in the town of Dumfries. On becoming bankrupt, Mr. Robert Ramsay, Writer & Banker in Dumfries, was appointed Trustee on McWhirter's estate, and was rather rigorous in making effectual a variety of small accounts, by actions before the Sheriff Court of Dumfries; in one of which, Professor Williamson was called for payment of a parcel of Stockings.—

On receiving the Summons, the Professor waited on his friend Dr. Muirhead, and requested either a loan to enable him to pay for the stockings, or a defence to be lodged in the Sheriff Court. The doctor told him that he preferred the defence; which accordingly he drew up in poetical numbers, of which a few verses only have been preserved in my memory.—

It began by stating an account of *debit* and *credit* between the Professor and MacWhirter; and after describing the valuable services which had been rendered to him and his family, whereby the Professor had shewn them the *road to Heaven,* he added—

"On t'other side per contra stand
Three pairs of stockings given.
When James McWhirter drew on God,
Far hence were all his ills,
More credit his petitions had
Than Ramsay's London Bills" &c.

This defence was lodged in the Sheriff Court by the professor; and, in Scottish Lawphrase, the claim for the stockings was *sopited.*—

Dr. Muirhead was of the *irritable genus,* and nowise disposed to submit to the abuse & sarcastic ballads of Burns, on whom he purposed to [hunt out of Society, as a public nuisance, and began to accomplish his purpose, partly *(deleted)*] retaliate by the same weapons Burns himself had made use of; whose lines on Elphinstones' *(sic)* Translation*s* *(sic)* of Martials' *(sic)* Epigrams[13] contain the following apostrophe to the Translator.

O thou, whom poesy abhors,
Whom prose has turned out of doors,
Heard'st thou that groan—&c.

One of these epigrams entitled *"In Vacceram quam malis artibus non locuptetatum, miratur"* is thus translated by Elphinstone—

Vile informer, slanders' *(sic)* child!
Dealer, who hast still beguil'd!
Shield of war, & soul of arms,
How hast thou no golden charms.

The original (of which the above is a most ridiculous translation) runs thus in Martial:—

Et delator es, et calumniator:
Et fraudator es, et negotiator:
Et *fellator* es, et Lanista: miror
Quare non habeas, Vacerra, nummos.

[13] r.d. deletes, "are excellent."

Dr. Muirheads' (*sic*) translation, levelled against Burns, refers to other epigrams which Martial had written upon Vacerra—

> Vacerra, shabby son of whore,
> Why do thy patrons keep thee poor?
> Bribe-worthy service, thou cans't boast
> At once their bulwark and their host.
> Thou art a sychophant and traitor,
> A liar, a calumniator;
> Who conscience—hadst thou that—would sell,
> Nay, lave the common shores of Hell
> For whiskey—Eke, most precious imp,
> Thou art a rhymster, *gauger,* pimp:
> Whence comes it then, Vacerra, that
> Thou still art poor as a church rat?

This and even more bitter effusions agt. Burns were printed by Dr. Muirhead for the purpose of circulation; of which a [great *(deleted)*] parcel was sent to me, and another [bundle *(deleted)*] to be given to Mr. Maxwell of Terraughty; which I presented to that gentleman, and after reading them over, he said that Burn's (*sic*) trash would be better answered by silence and contempt; and having thrown his own parcel into the fire, I followed his example with mine.—

Page 314.

I heartily wish the four paltry squibs against the Earl of Galloway had been omitted; for they not only have neither point nor merit of any kind, but are actually gross falsehoods dressed up in metre.—

His allusions to Lord Galloways' (*sic*) want of *courage*[14]

[14] Apparently a reference to this epigram:
> No Stewart are thou, Galloway,
> The Stewarts all were brave;
> Besides, the Stewarts were but fools,
> Not one of them a knave.

and *hospitality*[15] had not the remotest foundation in truth. His Lordship succeeded to a very embarrassed estate; which he retrieved by prudent management, and the knowledge which he had acquired of the whole country and its products, from constant residence during the best part of every year on his own property; where he was so far from living in a mean style, that he kept the best table, and had more guests, and saw more company, than all the rest of the County put together.

To impute *Cowardice* to his Lordship was also one of the most atrocious calumnies that could be invented. He was of a family of which an eminent Judge (Lord Kenyon) truly said, "all the Sons were brave and all the daughters virtuous." His Lordship's courage had been proved, on many occasions; and, in point of fact, Burns, who lived [an *(deleted)*] 100 miles distant from him, knew nothing about Lord G.—He knew as little of him as he did of his own patrons Lord Stair and Mr. Heron; who were opposed to his Lordship in election politics, and whom [he *(deleted)*] Burns was absurd [and foolish *(deleted)*] enough to consider as Whigs. His insinuation of Lord Galloway's want of Kindness, and his request to be spared his [Lop's *(deleted)*] *vengeance*,[16] are equally ridiculous; for Lord Galloway was

[15] Apparently a reference to this epigram:
> What dost thou in that mansion fair?—
> Flit, Galloway, and find
> Some narrow, dirty, dungeon cave,
> The picture of thy mind!

[16] A reference to the following epigram:
> Spare me thy vengeance, Galloway,
> In quiet let me live;
> I ask no kindness at thy hand,
> For thou hast none to give.

In this connection, it is appropriate to quote a passage from John Syme's letter to Alexander Cunningham, dated August 3, 1793. After recounting various adventures during his and Burns' tour of Galloway,

one of the kindest and most popular landlords in all the South of Scotland—beloved by the Tenants of his own paternal inheritance, and of the various [properties *(deleted)*] estates afterwards purchased by him, as well as by all his neighbours; and he was one of the firmest and most stedfast friends that ever existed.—

[Burns might very safely *deprecate* his vengeance: for I could have told him that when I mentioned to his Lop. what had passed between Terraughty and me, he said the old laird was a wise man; and as for himself, it would not

---

Syme tells of their being soaked by a storm and of their "vengeance at Gatehouse by getting utterly drunk." The next morning "Burns was quite discomfited—a sick stomach, headache &c lent their forces & the man of verse was quite *accablé*. Mercy on me how he did fume & rage—nothing would reinstate him in temper—I tried all I could think of, at length I got a lucky hit—across the bay of Wigton I showed him Ld. Galloway's house—He expectorated his spleen against the aristocratic elf, and regained a most agreeable temper— I have about half a dozen of capital extempores which I dare not write—But I may *repeat* and you shall hear them some time—I declare they possess as much point and classical *terseness* if I may so express myself, as anything I can imagine. O, he was in an epigrammatic humour indeed—I told him it was rash to crucify Ld. G—in the way he was doing for tho he might not receive any favours at his hands yet he might suffer an injury—He struck up immediately—
> Spare me thy vengeance G—ay
> In quiet let me live;
> I ask no kindness at thy hand
> For thou hast none to give."

It will be easily seen that here Burns was indulging his taste for epigrams, often more bitter than apt, and almost always unprovoked and recklessly imprudent. Cromek's descriptive phrase, repeated by later editors, "On The Author Being Threatened With His [Lord G's] Vengeance," is a mischievous interpolation. What can one say of Cunningham's note? "The sharp squibs were launched against the house of Galloway during the Heron contest. Though 'The Stewart' at first felt offended, he smiled, it is said, when he considered how way- ward the muse is, and how hot even the calmest blood grows during an election."

become him, when his good old master The King despised and disregarded the paltry attacks of a Peter Pindar, to feel himself hurt by those of a licentious, rhyming plough-man.—*(deleted)*]

P. 316.

Of the Epitaph on John Bushby I got a copy soon after it was made, from my friend Mr. John Syme; which was somewhat different from what is here printed—

"Here lies John Bushby, honest man!
Catch[17] him Devil, if ye can."—

I put it into the hands of Mr. Bushby as soon as it was received, and he merely laughed at it, seeming to think it rather complimentary, and said he would ask the fellow to dine with him some day at Tenwald downs, where I heard he went with his friend Mr. Syme, who was inti-mate with Mr. Bushby.—

That gentleman was at one time a Writer or an Attorney, but had given up [that *(deleted)*] practice long before the time of Burns. [Before *(deleted)*] & when Burns came to Dumfries Mr. Bushby held the lucrative office of Sherriff Clerk of the County, which disqualified him from prac-tising as a Writer or Attorney.—& he retained that office for all the rest of his life—He was not a man to be moved with such paper bullets; and if ever he had come in per-sonal conflict with the Bard, the latter, strong as he was, would have stood no chance whatever with Mr. B.—He on one occasion observed that he could not conceive why the poor devil had thought proper to run a muck against all those who could best do him a service, and none of whom, as far as he knew, held him at ill will.—

Mr. Bushby was factor or Steward on considerable estates

[17] Cunningham prints, "cheat."

both in Scotland and England; in which capacity he may not have been popular with the tenants, as is the case in general with factors, whether they deserve it or not; but I am sorry Mr. Cunningham, who appears to me to be impartial in general with regard to the merits and follies of Burns, should have received such bad information with regard to Mr. Bushby, as is contained in the following paragraph—"It is said that as he lay on his deathbed, "*knock* followed *knock* at his door, and *creditor* succeeded "*creditor* so fast, demanding money, that the sinking man "turned his face sullenly away, and muttered, they *winna* "let me die, by G—d!"[18]

Mr. Bushby did not reside in Dumfries, but at his villa of Tenwald-downs, some miles distant from it, where there could be no *knocks* at his door, nor would any *duns* or creditors have been admitted to disturb him in his dying moments. Besides, this paragraph contains intrinsic evidence of its falsehood; for he was a native of the north of England and always expressed himself in the broad English dialect of that country; the words *winna* and *canna* formed no part of his vocabulary. All that the Editor has detailed regarding this Gentn. is most incorrect & absurd.

But when Mr. Cunningham was making such a general *exposè* (*sic*) of the Works of Burns in this line, he might have included the following, written by him upon a relation of mine, Mrs. Young, formerly Mrs. Grizzel Craik, the widow of Thomas Young Esq. of Lincluden College, founded by Archibald the *Grim* Earl of Douglas—

> Here lies with Death, auld Grizzel *Grim*
> Lincluden's ugly witch,
> O Death! thou surely art not nice
> To lie with sic a b—ch.—

[18] A good example of Cunningham's creative editing; *cp*. Grierson notes, IV. Honest Allan here has embroidered the common gossip about *William* Bushby. r.d. gives Bushby's seat as Tinwald downs.

Page 72.

Robert Riddell of Glenriddell, so often mentioned in this Work with much applause, was my Schoolfellow, and in the same class with me at Dr. Chapmans' (*sic*) in Dumfries.

In that Class also were Dr. William Charles Wills of London, Dr. James Currie of Liverpool, Dr. George Bell of Manchester, Wm. Cunningham of Enterkin &c.; and I am sure it would have astonished all these as much as it does me, to read such praises of the most heavy, dull youth, the least of a Scholar, and the most incorrigible dolt[19] in our class. He did not come much forward into the World; after we quitted School,[20] I used to meet him at the Assizes and Dumfries Elections, when we always shook hands cordially, in remembrance of old Class fellowship; but that he should have been commemorated, as is done in these volumes, seems to me most extraordinary. I think the secret must have lain in his marrying an excellent and amiable lady of the name of Kennedy, whom all his old School fellows admired, as much as they under-valued him.[21]—

Page 111.

The *Heron* here mentioned[22] I became slightly acquainted with when I was a boarder in Dr. Blacklocks' (*sic*), and I always considered him to be a very disagreeable, conceited and ignorant person. On one occasion he brought to me

[19] r.d. deletes, "blockhead."

[20] r.d. deletes, "and I know no ill of him."

[21] Cunningham, with journalistic ease, dubbed Riddell "a distinguished antiquarian."

[22] In the poem "To Dr. Blacklock," dated Ellisland, 21st Oct. 1789. Robert Heron wrote a *Memoir* of Burns, the first extended account of him, in 1797. He knew Burns in Edinburgh and visited him at Ellisland. He was Dr. Blacklock's assistant, and later Dr. Hugh Blair's. The paragraph on Heron, and the preceding paragraphs on Robert Riddell and Mrs. Grizzel Craik, have been deleted.

(on the supposition of my being a good French Scholar, which I was not) a translation of Tales from the French similar to the Arabian Nights Entertainments, in which I found he had uniformly christened the word *Hotel* with the epithet of *Inn;* and on my noticing to him that he ought to leave it as it was—*Hotel,* or call it *house,* or *palace,* if he would translate it, he took his Manuscript away with him in great dudgeon; and though we met afterwards, we were never cordial, and he most justly considered me as a very indifferent Linguist.

Page 222.

The character of John Maxwell of Terraughty is admirably and truly given.[23] He was bred a Carpenter; and I have often heard him pique himself on his skill in that handcraft. It was, as he told me, the fashion of Scotch gentlemen at the time to breed up their younger Sons to such professions or trades, and that his friend and contemporary Sir George Clark Maxwell, sometime a Commissioner of the Customs, and afterwards Baronet, the Grandfather of the present Sir George of Pennycuik, was bred a *Wabster* i. e. a weaver.—

I have seen this excellent old man (Mr. Maxwell) in some particular Situations, and always had more and more reason to admire him—on one occasion I was present at a singular colloquy between him and one of his tenants of the name of David Brait; who wanted an extension of his lease for a considerable period, with an addition of more land; on which Mr. Maxwell said to the old man, "David! "ye've surely taen a *yeard* hunger; for to my knowledge, "ye're aboon fourscore"—to which David answered "that

[23] In the poem, "To John Maxwell of Terraughty, on his Birth-Day." The letter referred to at the end of this note on John Maxwell is not now with the memoir.

"comes weel frae you Laird; for to my knowledge ye're four "score and ten." What was the issue of the treaty I know not, but they parted very good friends.—See Letter "Being &.—

Page 201.

Miss Elizabeth Burnet, second daughter of Lord Monboddo, is frequently mentioned by Burns with great admiration, and most justly, for she was remarkably handsome and a very amiable young woman. She had one great personal defect however,—her teeth were much [decayed and *(deleted)*] discoloured, but fortunately she had a very small mouth, and took care not to open it much in mixed company. She was moreover, what is not noticed (either by the Poet or his Biographer) herself a poetess, and a very clever woman. She[24] & her Eldest Sister always accompanied their father on horseback, to and from Monboddo; their journey lying thro' the village of Laurence Kirk, erected in Kincardineshire by his friend and brother Judge Lord Gardenston, who was nearly, if not altogether, as eccentric a man as Lord M. himself.—

This Village was Lord Gardenston's hobbyhorse. He introduced many manufactures into it, and amongst others, the Snuff-boxes known by the name of the village, and still much admired. In the Inn which he established here, a large *Album* was kept, which was frequently enriched by quotations and donations from his own pen. The Miss Burnets in an idle hour[25] took occasion to insert a short address to his Lordship, imitated from the Prologue to the Rehearsal.—

[24] r.d. deletes, "rode beautifully on horseback and."
[25] r.d. deletes, "waiting till the horses were fed, (for her father abhorred the inside of any post chaise or [any *(deleted)*] other Vehicle)."

> "We well might call this bloated book of yours
> A poesy of weeds and not of flowers:
> Yet such have been presented to our noses,
> And some there are, I fear, who've thought them
> roses."—

Lord Gardenston, who frequently inspected his Album, was very irritable; and, taking offence at the above imitation, wrote below it with his own tremulous hand,

"This plagiary writer censures without sense: for though "there are some things in the Album improper, yet every "person will reap much entertainment from the variety of "quotations."

Which produced from the fair lady the following philippic—

> "My Lord, do not growl,
> 'Cause the verses are stole
> Altho' you smart under their lash;
> Should you purge your chaste olio
> Of each borrowed folio,
> I fear you'd leave little but trash.
> Yet, your Lordship should know,
> That a dangerous blow
> From no such a fair arm could come,
> For the stroke of a wand
> From a Lady's soft hand
> Is a compliment paid your *Album*.[26]
>
> Then dont take it ill
> That a feminine quill
> Has ventured to tickle your Toby;
> But allow her to urge,
> That, if you will purge,
> You first should consult Dr. Boby. x

X Dr. Robert Stewart of Fiddes, an eminent physician in Laurence Kirk.

[26] r.d. "A Gentn.—On being permitted to read this [act of *(deleted)*] *jeu d'esprit*, added—"*alii legunt, Auld-Bum*," which produced its immediate Consignation to the flames, from which being partly recovered, the rest was supplied by memory." This whole passage deleted.

X[27] Lord Monboddo certainly had not the reputation of giving the *most elegant entertainments*[28] in the northern metropolis as is said by Mr Cunningham. Many of his bretheren on the bench were far more remarkable in that line, tho' he was certainly hospitable, and gave [a great *(deleted)*] many dinners; [and *(deleted)*] That his apartments were decorated *with flowers of all hues* and his guests *regaled with music,* is no doubt true; for his two charming daughters were partial to music and Botany. The eldest, who was married to Mr. Kirkpatrick Williamson, tho' not so handsome as the second, was likewise a most amiable and accomplished young lady. But On the article of *Wines,* [his Lordship was as ignorant as a child. A

[27] The large X calls attention to an extended marginal note, as follows: "Since writing these notes chiefly from memory, I happened coming from Fort George to Perth to stop & dine at Laurence Kirk and on enquiring at the Landlord for Lord Gairnstone's Album he told me that it still existed & was often called for by travellers. I begged of him to bring it to me which he did, and sorry was I to find (July 1834) that it had been much disfigured & mutilated and latterly [much disfigured & *(deleted)*] I may say [even *(deleted)*] contaminated by worthless insertions [of low blackguard *(deleted)*] by a low sett of travellers—I had the happiness however to find the lines above quoted very complete and a copy of them was made by my daughter now the wife of Captn. Victor of the Royal Engineers.

I offered the Innkeeper five guineas for the remains of Lord Gairnstone's album, wh he declined, on grounds in which I could not possibly contest the validity, and on his telling me that the books [in *(deleted)*] and the library [in which they *(deleted)*] were [kept were *(deleted)*] in pretty good order, I took a cursory inspection of them, and made some enquiries at him respecting the present family of [the *(deleted)*] Garden of Troop, and their estate dont je fais peu de cas, and I presume others will do the same."

[28] A reference to Cunningham's remark, "He had the reputation of giving the most elegant entertainments during his day in the northern metropolis: he had flowers of all hues and wines of all qualities: odours as well as light were diffused by lamps, nor was his entertainments without the charm of music." See in this connection, Hope's remarks on Young's Memoir, *post.*

(deleted)][29] a Lawyer (Lop. Cullen) of his intimate acquaintance, who afterwards joined him on the Bench, told
me that Lord M. did not know Claret from Port; yet, that
being [one of the *(deleted)*] Counsel in the famous Douglas
Cause, and one of those who went to France, to take the
proofs in that country, he on his return dubbed himself a
great admirer and judge of Claret; and yet, [this gentleman
(deleted)] Mr Cullen assured me that he had seen a bottle
of Port imposed upon his Lordship as excellent Claret, and
recommended by him as such to a large company.—

I thought this at the time rather Apocryphal, but I afterwards had an opportunity of witnessing in person, that
great pretenders to judgment in Wine may very easily be
deceived. My friend Mr. John Irving of the Middle
Temple esteemed himself the greatest judge of Port in
Britain: but Sir Robert Herries, (who when he was a
banker in London was also a merchant in Barcelona) sent
Mr. Irving a present of some of the Wine of that [district
(deleted)] Country, as being excellent Port, and I saw some
of it presented at his table as such, and highly applauded
by Mr. Irving. But the hoax when discovered bred a cool-
ness betwixt these two parties, altho' Sir Robert pleaded
that it was a clear proof of Mr. Irving's judgment, for
Black Strap was a [wine *(deleted)*] much Superior wine to
Port; and with good reason might he say so, for when the
English were in possession of Toulon, Sir Robert cleared
several thousand pounds by cargoes of that wine, which
he transmitted to them from Barcelona.—

I am mistaken, however, in saying that the gentleman
who told me this anecdote of Lord Monboddo's judgment
in Wine afterwards joined him *on the Bench;* for his Lord-

[29] r.d. deletes, "and in most things the greatest bundle of quaint-
ness & unrivalled affectation that ever existed."

ship never sat on the Bench; he always took his seat at the table below, near the clerks of Session; [with the purpose, it *(deleted)*] and was [supposed, of *(deleted)*] render [ing *(deleted)*] ed [himself *(deleted)*] more conspicuous by his Crimson gown, in contrast with their black ones.—

Of his literature and classical knowledge I had at one time a great opinion; but I found that his clerk Mr. Hunter, afterwards Professor of Humanity in the University of Saint Andrews, was a [much *(deleted)*] greater Scholar than his Lordship. Of this I had convincing proofs afterwards. Having discovered that my Lord did not read Plato, or at least, did not quote Plato from the original Greek, but trusted entirely to translations, and even quoted from the errors of these translations, I conveyed an extract to his Lordship, who candidly acknowledged that he had quoted from the Latin translation of *Ficinus,* and the mistakes were the translators, not his. The proof of this, has been long preserved by me, and bears, "Lord Monboddo, in his origin and progress of languages vol. 2 p. 197, thus translates a passage of Plato's Cratylus [396d]—

"He (Socrates) says he had catched inspiration from Euthyphron, an enthusiast of those times, with whom he had conversed *that morning*"—

The original is εωθεν γαρ πολλα αυτω συνην (Ενθυνφρονω nempe) και παρειχον τα ωτα [*sic,* without accents]; which Ficinus thus translates. Illi siquidem astiti a *matutino* assiduis auresque porrexi. Does not his Lordship quote rather from Ficinus than Plato? He *tells* us he used this edition."

Page 304.

With Mr. John Syme of Ryedal I was intimately acquainted. He was the only son of Mr. John Syme W. S., who was Law agent for several of the principal families in

Galloway and wished to breed his son to the same profession; but the young man preferred the Army, from which he was prevailed upon by his father to sell out after a few years service; being still unable to conquer his aversion to the legal profession, he rather chose to follow agricultural pursuits; and having married and settled in Dumfries, he obtained the office of Collector of Stamps in that district. I recommended him as factor to my old Schoolfellow Dr. Currie of Liverpool, when he purchased the estate of Dumcrief in Annandale. And I likewise got him employed as factor to my client Wm. Neilson of Liverpool when he purchased the large estate of Newbie, belonging to the Marquis of Annandale. In consequence of my being the Law agent for these two estates, I had frequent intercourse with my friend Mr. Syme, who was an enthusiastic admirer of Burns, [though hardly more so than I was myself of his genius and talents; which, when I first knew him, I thought placed him in the same rank with Robert Fergusson, as a poet; but I soon came to be of opinion that he had far outstripped Fergusson.—*(deleted)*]

Mr. Syme frequently invited me to parties and jovial meetings at Dumfries with his friend Burns, but I must own I rather avoided his company; whilst at the same time I lamented the unfortunate situation in which he had been placed and the narrow circumstances in which he had *involved* himself; and on one occasion, when a client of mine—a shopkeeper in Dumfries—was *per*secuting [prosecuting *(correction)*] him for the price of a suit of Clothes & some furnishings to his family, I offered to Mr. Syme not only to ask indulgence, but also to pay the debt for him, which my friend advised me not to do, as the high spirit of Burns would not brook my interference in such a matter.—

[I had reason however to presume on a future occasion, when [he was near the end of his unhappy career and *(deleted)*] want and destitution pressed hard on him and his family, that, he had not been so fastidious and might have accepted, if not solicited, some assistance [from me *(deleted)*], which I for one would most willingly have given. *(This whole passage deleted)*]

I happened to be returning with my wife from London, and we meant to visit Dr. Muirhead, then at Spottes in Galloway; but Mrs. Young being taken ill, in place of proceeding to the doctor's residence, I wrote to him to meet and dine with us at Dumfries, so as we might proceed to Edinr. next day. Mr. Syme and Burns saw us as we stopped at the George Inn, and I remarked to my wife that poor Burns looked miserably ill. In a short time a message came to us, that Mr. Syme and Mr. Burns would be happy to dine with us. Expecting however Dr. Muirhead, I could not hazard the consequences of a meeting betwixt them, and of course sent our excuse.—[30]

This was the last time that I saw Burns; and Mrs. Young & I have ever since regretted that we had not accepted his offer of dining with us, and sent an express to Spottes to prevent Dr. Muirhead from coming to Dumfries.—

The next time that the Poet and his works were brought to my recollection was on finding my friend Dr. Currie

[30] r.d. deletes, "I had scarcely done so, when turning to the Window of the parlour in which we were, I saw on a pane of Glass the following lines on a noted character in Dumfries, a little hump [ed *(deleted)*]-backed, irascible, litigious lawyer of the name of *Glen*— [The words were *(deleted)*]
>David Glen, the best of little men
>Of the lawyer Kind *when drunk*

which [on being *(deleted)*] on a former occasion [being *(deleted)*] pointed out to Mr. Syme & Burns then present, the latter took out his diamond pen & added the words *Sober* or *drunk*"—

at Liverpool busily engaged in writing his Life; to which
he had been mainly induced by his factor Mr. Syme. The
Doctor put many questions to me regarding Burns, to which
I [begged him to be satisfied with *(deleted)*] generally made
one answer—"That I greatly admired the *Poet,* but dis-
liked the *Man.*"—

Since writing [some *(deleted)*] these notes on perusal of
the 3d. vol of Cunninghames' *(sic)* Life of Burns, I have
read the 8th, being the last volume of that work, containing remarks on Scottish Song, in which I think there are
several errors, but that upon the whole it is [the most curious volume of the Work—*(deleted)*] a valuable addn. to the
Life of Burns.

After some notice of the Song called "Bess the Gawkie,"
he adds, "Tradition ascribes the composition of this Song
'to *William Morehead* the minister of Urr, in Galloway:
'he was a maker of Verses, and falling under the lash of
'Burns, avenged himself by some satiric lines which have
'much ill nature but no wit."

The person here alluded to is evidently Dr. Jas. Muirhead
of Logan Minister at Urr [in Galloway *(deleted)*], some
notice of whom and his [political *(deleted)*] squabbles with
Burns will be found in my Notes on Vol. 3d. of this Work,—
Though the doctor wrote verses, he certainly was not so
good a Poet as Burns; but most assuredly he never intended
to measure his strength with him; He was not the aggressor
in his warfare with Burns, who without any provocation in
his doggerel election Ballads which had neither wit nor
merit of any kind that I could perceive [the doctor *(deleted)*] first attacked the Doctor who had a good right to
pay Burns in his own coin—and if, as the Editor says, [the
(deleted)] his Satirical lines had much ill nature but no
wit, they were the more on a par with those in which Burns

had previously [made an attack on him *(deleted)*] commenced this warfare. N L *(sic)* Altho' the late Mr. Maxwell of Terraughty, & I destroyed the copies that were sent to us of the doctors' *(sic)* verses, others were not so careful of the reputation and feelings of Robert Burns, and it consists with my knowledge that no publication in answer to the scurrilities of Burns ever did him so much harm in public opinion or made Burns himself feel so sore as Dr. Muirhead's translation of Martial's ode [of Vascera *(deleted)*] to Vacceras.—

When I remonstrated with the doctor against his printing and circulating that translation I asked him how he proved that Vacceras was *a gauger* as well as Burns, [to which *(deleted)*] he answered "Martial calls him Fellator, which means a Sucker or a man who drinks from the cask"—

p. 10   Roslyn Castle it is said was the production of [Roger Ewen *(deleted)*] Richard Hewit, a young man who was amanuensis to Dr. Blacklock. N. L. *(sic)* Intimate as I was with the doctor, and much as I admired these verses, I never heard of this anecdote before. But it is also said that Burns was indebted for the anecdote to Dr. Blacklock himself, and that he was on the most intimate & friendly footing with the Dr. [Blacklock *(deleted)*] on his first visit to Edinr. is unquestionable.—

I have still however some doubts on the subject, for it is added that Richard Hewit was the boy taken to lead the *blind* doctor during *his residence in Cumberland,* but according to my recollection he performed that office for the doctor in the town of Annan, where Dr. Blacklock's father was a Bricklayer. He may however have *led* the dr. both in Cumberland & [Ireland *(deleted)*] Annandale, but he was much more likely in the latter to have [had the *(deleted)*] heard Roslyn Castle & composed [for *(deleted)*] the verses which it is said he wrote for it.

p. 38　"There's nae luck about the House"—[There *(deleted)*] N. L. *(sic)* There is certainly an error in the Statement of this Ballad having first come on the streets in 1772, and that the composition of the Song was not much anterior to that period, for when I was at Annan School [anterior to this period *(deleted)*] some part at least of this beautiful Song was often [used *(deleted)*] sung by one of the maid servants of the Revd. Mr. Wm. Wright our master, afterwards minister of Newabbey. And the boys of Mr. Wrights' *(sic)* Academy used often to prevail on her to Sing it to them with other favorite Scotch Songs by which they were originally impressed on my memory—[31]

p. 59　"Bide ye yet."

It consists with my knowledge that this Song was composed by the lady here mentioned,[32] for I have heard her sing it, as well as an other Song [s *(deleted)*] of her own composition, but the Account given of her in this compilation contradicts all my knowledge both of this lady, her talents and family; and yet of these I ought to have a pretty accurate knowledge, inasmuch as I was well acquainted with her from my infancy till very near the period of her death—[33]

[31] Young here pushes back the composition of this song possibly twenty years. He was a young man just beginning practice in 1786; he is writing in 1834; his schooling in Annan must have been in the 1760's. Burns places the composition of the song "long posterior to Ramsay's days," and says, "about the year 1771, or 72, it came first on the streets as a ballad."

[32] Miss Jenny Graham, of Dumfries.

[33] Cunningham's lively "account" is as follows: "The authoress was

Miss Jenny Graham was one of the daughters of Graham of Shaw, an old and respectable family in Annandale in the parish of Hutton and [Covan *(deleted)*] Cowie, of which my father and grandfather were ministers for a period of 75. years.—

During the time of being at School both at Annan and Dumfries, I frequently saw Miss [Jenny *(deleted)*] Graham [of Shaw *(deleted)*], and early conceived a high respect for her, as eminent in talents & qualifications above what [generally *(deleted)*] often fall [s *(deleted)*] to the lot of her sex. She was a good Poetess and had a great deal of humour. When I first knew her, she resided chiefly at Westerhall with Lady Johnstone, who was the sister of Patrick Lord El [l *(deleted)*] ibank, the mother of Sir James Johnstone and Sir Wm. Pulteney, and a person of extraordinary and rare endowments. Miss Graham was one of the prime favorites of this lady till the day of her death. I afterwards knew Miss Graham when I was a boarder at Dr. Chapman's the master of the Grammar School at Dumfries. She then resided in the family of Major Walter Johnstone, brother to Sir James Johnstone of Westerhall, who was one of the original [bankers *(deleted)*] partners of Messrs. Johnstone Lawson & Company, by whom Bank Notes were first issued in Dumfries. I had the honor of being invited some times to dine at this gentlemans' *(sic)*

---

a maiden lady; she lived to a good old age and died of an asthma, the pain of which she alleviated in composing humourous Scottish songs. She was a fine dancer in her youth; a young nobleman was so much charmed with her graceful movements, and the music of her feet, that he enquired in what school she was taught. 'In my mother's washing tub,' was the answer." It would seem that here as elsewhere, Cunningham's narrative is more picturesque than reliable.

house on Saturdays, and [on one occasion *(deleted)*] I shall never forget a scene at which I happened to be present. N L. The Major had a very bad practice of cursing & swearing at his Servants, especially for any blunders or mistakes committed by them when [they were *(deleted)*] waiting at Table—He had on one occasion poured forth such a torrent of abuse and malediction against an unfortunate Annandale youth who had incurred his displeasure, that I expected Miss Graham would rebuke him for it, but on the contrary she added such a [pale *(deleted)*] peal of curses to the Majors as astonished the whole company & none more than the Major himself, who burst into a fit of laughter when she proposed to desist from such an unseemly practice if he would promise to do the same and I was told several years thereafter that he was hardly ever known thencefurth *(sic)* to swear at or curse a [single *(deleted)*] a *(sic)* servant. [thereafter *(deleted)*]

Miss Graham resided in Edinr. when I attended the College there [afterwards *(deleted)*], and some of her nearest relations (Miss Bell of Crurie and others) then lived with her. I remember her complaining occasionally of an indifferent state of health, but that in alleviation of the pains of *Asthma* she composed *humourous* Scottish Songs I regard [to be *(deleted)*] as sheer nonsense, altho' I know that she did actually write several pieces of humour, not however to be Sung, but to be recited and to raise a laugh in company and I have heard the late Dr. [Samuel *(deleted)*] John Rogerson (who was the Son of a small farmer in the same parish with Mr. Graham of Shaw, the father of Miss Graham), rehearse some of her poems of a very humorous nature, and on one of these occasions I took the liberty of remarking to the doctor that his remembrance of our old friend Miss Graham proved that she was a better Poetess than similar recollections did of his great friend & patroness the Empress Catherine of Russia.—

That Miss Graham was *a fine dancer*—"had *charmed a young nobleman by her graceful move*ments—and told him she *had acquired them in her Mothers' wash*ingtub," I am satisfied must appear to all those who knew her as well as I did, to be arrant nonsense, having no foundation whatever in truth.

p. 67. "Fife and a' the lands about it."

Is said to have been composed by Dr. Blacklock and [tho' *(deleted)*] Burns certainly had good access to know what Songs were written by the doctor; but I knew the doctor in early life, before Burns ever saw him, and I cannot subscribe to the censure & severity of his criticisms on some of the Songs composed by [the *(deleted)*] doctor Blacklock and his poems in general. He was blind and if not actually born so, had no recollection of having ever enjoyed the blessings of sight, but yet he described natural objects and the feelings of mankind in general in a most vivid and [pleasant *(deleted)*] pleasing style, and making allowance for his want of sight, I humbly think some of his Songs will bear comparison with the best of those [Songs *(deleted)*] that were written by Burns himself.

125 "Whistle and I'll come to you my Lad."

In reference to this Song, as composed by Dr. Blacklock, it is said "The blind bard had a fine ear 'but external nature had begun to fade and grow 'dim in his remembrance." No wonder that it should, [when he was *(deleted)*] he being merely an infant when he lost his sight, which never supplied his descriptions. These were taken from other Writers, and in general were remarkably correct—.

Dr. Blacklock not only composed several good Songs but likewise sung his own compositions in a most scientific, pleasing style, accompanied by the *psalter,* an instrument on which he played with great taste and skill, until a paralytic affection in his hands, which had taken place before Burns knew him, made him lay aside that instrument & desist from those recitations which were so agreeable to all his boarders & pupils, & which were admired even by the celebrated Dr. Samuel Johnstone ["t" and "e" *(deleted)*].

I cannot think that justice is done to Dr. Blacklock in this work, and yet he was one of the best friends and sincerest admirars *(sic)* Burns ever had.—

106. "The Highland or 42d Regiments' March"—

It is said was composed by "Sir Harry Erskine, *a wit, orator, and poet."* He was a well informed, agreeable gentleman, and author of some *minor* poetry, but I never before heard that he was either a wit or an orator. I knew him only as the Honble Mr. H. Erskine brother to the Earl of Kellie[34] [originally "Kelly"].

146. "The Tears I shed must ever fall"—

"This Song it is said was composed by *A* Miss Cranston."

I should be glad to know if Mrs. Dugald Stewart,

[34] Young's marginal note: "In this note I find I have fallen into an Error, as to the Author of the 'Garb of old Gaul &c, which has been most obligingly Corrected by The Lord President The Right Honl Chas Hope."

the lady here meant, acknowledges this performance, and recognizes the description given of her by Burns, who certainly lay under greater obligations to her husband than to all the rest of the World.—But I shall pursue this Subject no longer. That Burns was [really *(deleted)*] a great poet, and an extraordinary man, seems to me unquestionable; but the abuse of his country and countrymen, for not bestowing on him a greater share of praise and patronage [and of comfortable *(deleted)*] with more comfort and independence than he actually enjoyed, [may well in my opinion be easily refuted and *(deleted)*] in my humble opinion admits of the most satisfactory contradiction.—

V

THE HOPE MANUSCRIPT

V

THE HOPE MANUSCRIPT

Robert Burns[1]

I met Burns several times at dinner in different Houses, when he first came to Edinr but I was not at all intimate with Him That visit of his to Edinr was a great misfortune to him, & led to all his after follies & misconduct, & ultimately to his ruin & premature death—to all of which his Intimacy with Nicol mainly contributed—Nicoll, as you say, was a good Scholar, but I did not consider him as a *better* Scholar than Adam or Fraser—His passions were quite ungovenable (*sic*), & He was altogether a most unprincipled Savage—He persecuted poor Adam by every means in his power; & at last was guilty of a brutal Assault on him, for which the Magistrates did not expell him, as they ought to have done—As a specimen of Nicols unprincipled disposition, & at the same time of his Selfish cunning, take the following Anecdote—You Know it was at that time the Custom for the Rector once a Week to go & examine the Class of one of the other Masters, who, at the same time, came into the Rectors Class & examined it—On one of those ocasions (*sic*), when I was Dux of the Rectors Class, Nicol came to examine us—. He seemed to be in particular good

[1] Lord Granton's title.

humour, anticipating, I have no doubt, the triumph he expected over the Rector—He went on for some time in the usual way, hearing us translate & construe—He then began to put some difficult questions, which Several of the Boys could not answer, but on putting them to me & other boys at the Head of the Class, they were all answered—At last He put a question which neither I nor any other Boy could answer—On which He turned to me & said, You are a pretty fellow, Sir to be at the Head of this School—not to be able to answer this question—I'll show you that your Cousin John Hope (the late Lord Hopetoun) in my Class can answer it, & make you ashamed of yourself—He then called the Janitor & desired Him to call John Hope to come to Him—John came & the Question was put to him, but John could not answer it—Nicol was evidently very angry, but He had the Selfish Cunning not to outrage the Son of Such a Man as Old Lord Hopetoun— So He merely desired Hope to go away & send Elliott, the Heriotter, to Him—Accordingly Elliott came, & the question was repeated to him, but He did not answer it either, on which the Savage lost all command of himself, flew at poor Elliott, seized & shook by both Ears, till He almost tore them off, & quite forgetting himself, exclaimed You Scoundrel, Have not I been dunning this into you for a week past—showing that He had been leading his Boys out of their depth, & attempting to make them get by rote things they did not understand, in hopes of having it to say, that His Boys only in the third Class were farther advanced than the Rectors—This explosion operated like Electricity on the Class—There was a universal shout & Hiss, & we all ran out of the school, leaving Nicoll frantic but stupefied with rage—So much for Nicol

Mr. Heron—I agree with you as to your Character of

this amiable Gentleman, & I don't believe a word of his alledged Suicide—Indeed I never heard a Surmise of it at the time, or indeed till I read it in your Memoir—I don't know if you ever heard of the Maneuvre, by which He carried His return at the Election to which you allude—If not, I will tell it you, for it cannot be so well described on paper.

Mr Maxwell of Munches—
His letter which you quote, is so curious as to the state of the Country in his Youth, & so curious considering his age at the time of writing it, then 91 that it is a pity it is not published.

Lord Monboddo—I was very well acquainted with Lord M. & rather a favorite of his, which originated in the following Circumstance, Characteristic of his peculiar turn—I was in a hearing in presence very soon after I came to the Bar—When I had finished my Speech, Lord Monbo. came up & was pleased to compliment me on my appearance—& Said I perceive, Mr Hope, that you have been educated in England—may I ask at what School—I told him—Did you learn Greek there? I said Yes We began the Greek Grammar at the same time with the Latin, & carried on both Languages together—Aye, there is the thing, said Monboddo, & now I suppose You can read Greek almost as well as you can do English—Why I said, my Lord I am sorry to say that I have forgot a good deal of my Greek since I came to Scotland—Aye, there is the thing again now—Mr Hope will you do me the honor to sup with me to night—He was better pleased to hear that I had partly forgot Greek in Scotland, than that I had learned it England (*sic*), for it suited his Theory as to the proficiency of the two Countries in that Language—And at Supper He prelected on me & my information & I was a great favorite—If I had time, I

believe I could furnish a pretty good Collection of Mon-
boddiana—One I recollect just now, which will give you a
Specimen of his peculiar fancies, & of the Force & Epigra-
matic (*sic*) manner in which He expressed himself—At one
of his Suppers (for it was always Supper parties that He
had, never dinners) He began the usual Subject of the
degeneracy of Mankind, which He exemplified thus—Look
at the President (Dundas) a tolerable sized Man—Look at
his Son the Soliciter (*sic*)—There is the Justice Clerk
(Miller) a good portly person—Look at his son Willy
Miller—And even Lord Alva *has contrived* to get a Son
less than himself—

On another Occasion, having started the same Subject,
One of the party asked him, what Height He Supposed
Achilles to have been—Why, said He, Achilles I think could
not have been less than 10 or 12 feet high—Upon which I
said, then I think we can have a good guess as to the Size
of the generality of the Greeks—for Achilles is said by
Homer to have been the Head & Shoulders Taller than
Ajax, & that Ajax was a Head & Shoulders taller than any
other man in the Army—Now if you deduct Two Heads &
Shoulders of such Men, it wont leave above 6 feet as the
height of the other Greeks—Monboddo did not like this
remark, & I was rather out of favor for a week or two—

What you say of Miss Burnett is quite correct—Her teeth
were not good—& she was not very well made below—She
had very thick Clumsy Ancles, which She was at the pains
to conceal by wearing her petticoats uncommonly long—
& she was not a good Dancer—but take her all in all was a
beautiful Creature—

I have no doubt that her Father hastened her fate, by
his folly in attempting to make her too hardy, by accom-
panying him, on all his Journeys (except to London) on
Horseback—As a specimen of his Absurdity in his treatment

of her—I was at a Ball & Supper given by Mrs Dundas at
Arniston, in the Xmas Holidays, 1784-5 or 85.6 I forget
which—Miss B danced a good deal, & the room was crowded
& hot—We went to supper about 12 oClock—When Miss B
was missing—On which Mrs. Dundass (sic) exclaimed—
Surely the Monster has not carried her off—Charles, to me,
run & see—So I went & I actually found Her Father and
She in the Stable Yard, mounting their Horses to ride
back to Edinr—so I took forcible possession of his Daughter,
& brought her back to a warm Supper & Bed, leaving Mono
—to prosecute his ride if He chose—& I have no doubt, that
this prolonged her life; for heated as She was, that ride
must have killed her

Whether Lord M was himself a good Judge of Wine, I
do not know—But this I know, that his Wine was always
excellent especially his Claret—This He treated in a peculiar
way—He always bought it in the Cask—& then cased, & put
it into a Hot House—where it ripened in a few months
more than it would have done in as many Years in Bottles.
Sometimes He used to have a Magnum of Claret brought
in with a Chaplet of Flowers round the Neck of it—He
always mixed a few drops of Seltzer Water with His Claret,
as He said it was a Mark of Debauchery among the Ancients
to drink their wine unmixed with Water—Nay he insisted
that they used to mix *Sea* Water with it—This He grounded
on a passage in one of the poets (I forget which) who
speaks of *Vinum Expers Maris*—We endeavoured to per-
suade Him that this only meant Vin de paix, which had
not been imported by Sea from abroad—But He would not
be convinced, but said He did not approve of *Sea* Water,
& preferred *Seltzer*—

Lord Monboddo was an excellent Horseman, & a Keen
Fox Hunter, & being exceedingly Shortsighted, He often got
into very dangerous Scrapes—He had a famous Horse,

which he called *Alborac,* after the Horse of the Prophett
(*sic*) —On one occasion, in following the Hounds, He attempted a leap which, if he had seen the exact nature of it,
He probably would not have ventured—The consequence
was, that Alborac & He fell & tho Lord M escaped, poor
Alborac broke his Neck—& Old John Davidson, who was an
Excellent Scholar, & a great friend of Monboddo's, wrote a
Latin Epitaph on Alborac—I forget the whole of it, but
the point was, "Qui suam frangendo, vix Domini collam
servavit"—

Sir Henry Erskine was certainly the author of the words
of the March of the 42d Regt—In the garb of old Gaul &c—
Whether He also composed the Music, I do not know—But
you confound him with the facetious Andrew Erskine,
brother of Lord Kelly, who afterwards drowned himself a
little way from my house at Granton—Sir Harry Erskine was
not of the Kelly but of the Buchan family He was son of
Sir Charles who was Son of Sir John, a Brother of Lord
Buchan—In fact He was Sir Harry Erskine of Alva, but was
obliged to sell that Estate, which was purchased by his
Brother the Justice Clerk Tinwald—who was Succeeded in it
by Lord Alva, who again Sold Alva to Mr Johnstone—Sir
Harry was a General Officer, & Colonel of the 42d, &
married a Sister of Wedderburn afterwards Lord Rosslyn
by whom He was Father of the present Lord Rosslyn—Sir
Harry died about the year 1765—when his Son this Lord
Rosslyn was only 3 years Old—He was a great favorite of
George 3d in his Younger days, & succeed (*sic*) my Relation Sir William Breton as privy purse to the King—I
never heard whether Sir Harry ever composed any other
Lyrical Effusions except the march of the 42d—but poor
Andrew Erskine composed many—& was really a Wit & a
great companion of Sir John Whiteford, Matthew Hendes-
son (*sic*) & all that set—

VI

THE JOURNAL OF THE
BORDER TOUR

VI

THE JOURNAL OF THE BORDER TOUR

Introductory Note

The only occasions on which Burns is known to have kept a regular journal were his tour of the Border in May, 1787, and his visit to the Highlands in the late summer of the same year. Dr. Currie, the poet's first authorized biographer, made some slight use of these documents, but what was alleged to be the complete text was first published by Allan Cunningham in 1834, after being further quoted by Lockhart in his *Life of Burns* in 1828. When the original of the Highland journal again came to light some years ago it proved to be considerably briefer than Cunningham's printed text. Mr. J. C. Ewing, who in 1927 edited the work in facsimile, believes the additions to have been made by Burns himself in a recension, now lost, of his original penciled notes. Professor Snyder regards Cunningham himself as the author of the revisions.[1] In the absence alike of Burns' enlarged manuscript and of any proof that such a manuscript ever existed, Snyder's conclusion is the only one that makes sense. Cunningham's reputation as editor and biographer is so justly suspect that the burden of proof rests upon the defenders of his text.

[1] F. B. Snyder, *Life of Robert Burns* (New York, 1932), pp. 244 and 254 *note*.

The printed text of the Border journal remains as Cunningham published it. The original manuscript is now in the possession of Lt.-Col. Sir John Murray, D.S.O., of London, to whom I am indebted for permission to use a photostatic copy. The manuscript was bequeathed in 1873 to Sir John's grandfather by Mr. Hope Scott of Abbotsford, whose father had received it from Lockhart himself. Comparison with Cunningham's text reveals no rewriting and expansion such as the Highland journal suffered. Instead, we find Cunningham omitting several hundred words, though at the close he gives three entries which are not now, and apparently never were, with the rest of the journal. The main text, moreover, is followed by fourteen pages of miscellaneous memoranda, some of which, like the omitted passages of the diary itself, have biographical significance.

In its present state the journal comprises fifty-seven pages, octavo in size and all written in ink except a few of the miscellaneous notes at the end. Nine leaves at the beginning have been torn out—the act, Sir John states, of someone to whom his grandfather rashly lent the book. Initial letters remaining on the stubs of these leaves indicate that they contained verse which must have totaled ninety or a hundred lines. Occasionally a whole monosyllable, such as "To," "An'," "For" or "With" remains, but it is impossible to identify the missing material with any of Burns' published work. In all likelihood it was some of his "cloaciniad" verse, and fell victim to an attack of Victorian righteousness.

In December, 1934, I published in *PMLA*[2] the greater part of Cunningham's omissions, with such information as

[2] Vol. xlix, pp. 1107-15. My opening paragraphs, above, are from that article, somewhat condensed.

I had been able to collect about the people and places mentioned. Those tentative and incomplete notes I do not care to reprint. The ideal edition of the Journal would be fully annotated and accompanied by a facsimile. But I can aspire neither to the Scottish sojourn requisite for preparing such an edition nor to the Scottish patronage requisite for publishing it. Hence I gladly take this opportunity of at least making available the complete and undoctored text, and of modestly adding myself to the long list of editors who have shirked the job of annotation.

Cunningham suppressed no important biographical data, yet the Burns of his text is a less solid figure than the peasant of genius who filled his journal with the materials for future erotic reveries, suffered increasing boredom from heavy farmers, and saw through the pretensions of patronizing gentry. This is too self-conscious to be a great journal but it is essential Burns, and it adds one more to the growing list of documents in which the poet has a chance to speak for himself without the intervention of an editor equipped with scissors, eraser, and a moral pocket-handkerchief to hold before his streaming eyes.

DeLancey Ferguson

Western Reserve University

The Journal of the Border Tour

May 6th

Left Edin^r. [*May 5*]— Lammermuir hills miserably dreary
but at times very picturesque— Lanton edge a glorious
view of the Merse—reach Berrywell—Old M^r. Ainslie an
uncommon character—his hobbies Agriculture natural
philosophy & politics— In the first he is unexceptionably
the clearest-headed, best-informed man I ever met with; in
the other two, very intelligent— As a Man of business he
has uncommon merit, and by fairly deserving it has made
a very decent independance— Mrs Ainslie an excellent,
sensible, chearful, amiable old woman—Miss Ainslie an
angel—her person a little of the embonpoint but handsome
her face, particularly her eyes full of sweetness and good
humour—she unites three qualities rarely to be found together, keen, solid penetration; sly, witty observation and
remark; and the gentlest, most unaffected female Modesty—
Douglas, a clever, fine promising young fellow— The family
meeting with their brother, my compagnion [*sic*] de voyage,
very charming, particularly the sister—

The whole family remarkably attached to their menials—
M^{rs} A—full of stories of the sagacity & sense of the little

girl in the kitchen—M^r A—high in the praises of an African, his house servant— All his people old in his service—Douglas's old Nurse came to Berrywell yesterday to [tell *(deleted)*] remind them of its being Douglas's birth day—

A Mr Dudgeon, a Poet at times, a worthy, remarkable character—[a good deal of *(deleted)*] natural penetration, a great deal of information, some genius, and extreme Modesty—

Sunday—went to church at Dunse—D^r. Bowmaker a man of strong lungs and pretty judicious remark; but ill skilled in propriety, and altogether unconscious of his want of it— Monday [*May 7*]—Coldstream—went over to England— Cornhill—glorious river Tweed—clear & majestic—fine bridge—dine at Cold^m. with M^r. Ainslie & Mr Foreman—beat M^r F— in a dispute about Voltaire—tea at Lenel house with Mr Bryden— Mr Brydon a man of quite ordinary natural abilities, ingenious but not deep, chearful but not witty, a most excellent heart, kind, joyous & benevolent but a good deal of the French indiscriminate complaisance—from his situation past & present an admirer of every thing that bears a splendid title or possesses a large estate— Mrs Brydon a most elegant woman in her person and manners, the tones of her voice remarkably sweet— My reception from M^r. & M^{rs}. Brydon extremely flattering— Sleep at Coldstream—

Tuesday [*May 8*]—breakfast at Kelso—charming situation of Kelso—fine bridge over Tweed—enchanting views & prospects on both sides of the river, particularly the Scotch side; introduced to Mr Scot of the royal bank—an excellent modest fellow—visit Roxburgh Palace—fine situation of it—ruins of Roxburgh castle—a holly bush growing where James 2^d of Scotland was accidently killed by the bursting of a cannon—a small old religious ruin and a fine old garden planted by the religious, rooted out and destroyed by an English hottentot, a Maitre d'hotel of the Duke's, a M^r. Cole, climate & soil of Berwick shire & even Roxburgh shire superiour to Ayrshire—bad roads—turnip & sheep husbandry their great improvements—M^r. M^cdowall at Caverton mill a friend of M^r. Ainslie's, with whom I dined today, sold his sheep, ewe & lamb together, at two guineas a piece—wash their sheep before shearing—7 or 8 lb of washen wool in a fleece—low markets, consequently low rents—fine lands not above 16 sh Scotch acre—Magnificence of Farmers & farm houses—came up Teviot & up Jed to Jedburgh to lie, & so wish myself goodnight.

Wedensday [*May 9*]

Breakfast with M^r. Fair in Jedburgh a blind man but the first man of business as a Writer in town—a squabble between M^rs F—, a craz'd, talkative Slattern and a sister of hers an old maid, respecting a relief Minister—Miss gives Madam the lie, & Madam by way of revenge upbraids her that she laid snares to entangle the said minister, then a widower, in the net of matrimony—go about two miles out of Jedburgh to a roup of Parks—meet a polite soldier-like gentleman, a Captn. Rutherford who had been many years thro the wilds of America, a prisoner among the Indians—

Charming, romantic situation of Jedburgh, with gardens, orchards, &c. intermingled among the houses—fine old ruins, a once magnificent Cathedral [and strong castle *(deleted)*]— All the towns here have the appearance of old, rude grandeur; but extremely idle—Jed a fine romantic little river—

Dine with Captn. Rutherford. The Captn. a specious polite fellow, very fond of money in his farming way, but showed a particular respect to My Bardship—his lady exactly a proper matrimonial second part for him—Miss Ruther-

ford a beautiful girl, but too far gone woman to expose so
much of so fine a swelling bosom—her face tho' very fine
rather inanimately heavy—return to Jedburgh—walk up
Jed with some ladies to be shown Love-lane & Black-burn
two fairy scenes—introduced to Mr Potts, Writer, a very
clever fellow; & Mr Somerville the clergyman of the place,
a man & a gentleman, but sadly addicted to punning— The
walking Partie of ladies—M^{rs} F— & Miss Lookup her sister
before-mentioned. N.B. these two appear still more comfortably ugly & stupid, and bore me most shockingly—
[The *(deleted)*] Two Miss Fairs, tolerably agreable but
too much of the Mother's half-ell [features *(deleted)*] mouth
& hag-like features—Miss Hope, a tolerably pretty girl, fond
of laughing & fun—Miss Lindsay a good-humor'd amiable
girl; rather short et embonpoint, but handsome and extremely graceful—beautiful hazle eyes full of spirit &
sparkling with delicious moisture—an engaging face &
manner, un tout ensemble that speaks her of the first order
of female minds—her sister, a bonie, strappan, rosy, sonsie
lass— Shake myself loose, after several unsuccessful efforts,
of M^{rs}. F—r & Miss L—p and somehow or other get hold
of Miss Lindsay's arm—my heart thawed into melting pleasure after being so long frozen up in the Greenland bay of
Indifference amid the noise and nonsense of Edin^r.— Miss
seems very well pleased with my Bardship's distinguishing
her, and after some slight qualms which I could easily mark,
she sets the titter round at defiance, and kindly allows
me to keep my hold; and when parted by the ceremony of
my introduction to Mr Somerville she met me half to
resume my [hold *(deleted)*] situation— Nota Bene—The
Poet within a point and a half of being damnably in love—
I am afraid my bosom still nearly as much tinder as ever—
    The old, cross-grained, whiggish, ugly, slanderous hag,

Miss Lookup with all the poisonous spleen of a disappointed, ancient maid, stops me very unseasonably to [fall abusively foul *(deleted)*] ease her hell-rankling bursting breast by falling [foul *(deleted)*] abusively foul on the Miss Lindsays, particularly my Dulcinea; I hardly refrain from cursing her to her face— May she, for her pains, be curst with eternal desire and damn'd with endless disappointment! Hear me, O Heavens, and give ear, O Earth! may the burden of antiquated Virginity crush her down to the lowest regions of the bottomless Pit! for daring to mouth her calumnious slander on one of the finest pieces of the workmanship of Almighty Excellence. Sup at M[r]. F— vexed that the Miss Lindsays are not of the supper party as they only are wanting—M[rs]. F—r & Miss L—p still improve infernally on my hands—

Set out next morning [*May 10*] for Wauchope the seat of my correspondent M[rs]. Scot—breakfast by the way with D[r]. Elliot an agreable, good-hear[ted] climate-beaten, old veteran in the medical line; now retired to a romantic but rather moorish place on the banks of the Roole—he accompanies us almost to Wauchope—we traverse the country to the top of Bonchester, the scene of an old encampment, & Woolee hill—

Wauchope— M[r]. Scot exactly the figure [commo *(deleted)*] and face commonly given to Sancho Pança—very shrewd in his farming matters and not unfrequently stumbles on what may be called a strong thing rather than a good thing, but in other respects a compleat Hottentot— M[rs]. S— all the sense, taste, intrepidity of face, & bold, critical decision which usually distinguish female Authors— Sup with M[r] Potts—[a fine (?) *(deleted)*] agreable Partie—Breakfast next morning [*May 11*] with M[r] Sommerville—the bruit of Miss Lindsay and my Bard-

ship by means of the invention & malice of Miss L—p— Mr
Sommerville sends to Dr Lindsay begging him & family
to breakfast [but at all ev *(deleted)*] if convenient, but at
all events to send Miss L— accordingly Miss L— only
comes— I find Miss L— would soon play the devil with
me—I meet with some little flattering attentions from her—

Mrs S— an excellent, motherl[y], agreable woman, and
a fine famil[y]—Mr. Ainslie & Mr. S— Junrs. with Mr. Fair,
Miss Lindsay and me, go to see Esther, a very remarkable
woman for reciting Poetry of all kinds, and sometimes
making Scotch doggerel herself— She can repeat by heart
almost every thing she has ever read, particularly Pope's
Homer from end to end—has studied Euclid by herself,
and in short is a woman of very extraordinary abilities—
on conversing with her I find her fully to come up to the
character given of her—She is very much flattered that I
send for her, and that she sees a Poet who has put out a
book as she says— She is, among other things, a great
Florist—and is rather past the meridian of once celebrated
beauty but alas! tho very well married, before that period
she was violently suspected for some of the tricks of the
Cytherean Déesse—

I walk down Esther's garden with Miss L— and after
some little chit-chat of the tender kind I presented her
with a proof-print of my nob, which she accepted with
something more tender than gratitude— She told me many
little stories which Miss L—p had retailed concerning her
and me, with prolonging pleasure—God bless her!

Was waited on by the Magistrates and presented with
the freedom of the burgh—

Took farewell of Jedburgh with some melancholy, dis-
agreable sensations— Jed, pure be thy chrystal streams,
and hallowed thy sylvan banks! Sweet Isabella Lindsay,

may Peace dwell in thy bosom, uninterrupted, except by the tumultuous throbbings of rapturous Love! That love-kindling eye must beam on another, not me; that graceful form must bless another's arms, not mine!—

Kelso—dine with the farmer's club—all gentlemen, talking of high matters—each of them keeps a hunter from 30 to 50 £ value, and attend the fox-huntings in the country—go out with Mr Ker. one of the club, [to lie *(deleted)*] and a friend of M^r. Ainslie's, to lie— Mr Ker a most gentleman[l]y, clever, handsome fellow, a widower with some fine children—his mind & manner astonishingly like my dear old friend Robert Muir in Kilmarnock—every thing in M^r. Ker's most elegant—he offers to accompany me in my English tour—dine next day [*May 12*], a devilish wet day, with Sir Alex^r. Don—Sir A. D. a pretty clever fellow but little in him—far, far from being a match for his divine lady—poverty & pride the reigning features of the family—lie at Stodrig again; and set out [*Sunday, May 13*] for Melrose—visit Dryburgh, a fine old ruined Abbey, by the way— Still bad weather—cross Leader & come up Tweed to Melrose—dine there and visit that far-fam'd, glorious ruins— Come to Selkirk, up Ettrick the whole country [on T *(deleted)*] hereabout, both on Tweed and Ettrick, remarkably stony—
Monday [*May 14*]—

Come to Inverleithing a famous Spaw, & in the vicinity of the palace of Traquair, where having dined, and drank some Galloway-whey, I here remain till tomorrow—saw Elibanks & Elibraes so famous in baudy song today—on the other side of Tweed—
Tuesday [*May 15*]

drank tea yesternight at Pirn with Mr Horseburgh. Breakfasted today with Mr Ballantine of Hollowlee— Pro-

posal for a four-horse team to consist of M^r. Scot of
Wauchope Fittie-land; Logan of Logan Fittie-furr; Ballan-
tine of Hollowlee Forewynd; Hor[se]burgh of Horseburgh
Forefurr— Dine at a country Inn, kept by a Miller, in
Earlston, the birth-place and residence of the celebrated
Thomas A Rhymer—saw the ruins of his castle— Come to
Berrywell—

Wedensday [*May 16*]—dine at Dunse with the farmer's
club— Company—impossible to do them justice—Rev^d. M^r
Smith a famous Punster and Mr Meikle a celebrated Me-
chanic and inventor of the threshing-mills—lie again at
Berrywell— Thursday [*May 17*] breakfast at Berrywell &
walk into Dunse— To see a famous knife made by a Cutler
in Dunse and to be presented to an Italian Prince— A
pleasant ride with my friend Mr Robt Ainslie & his angelic
sister to Mr Thomson's a man who has newly commenced
farmer, & has married a Miss Patty Grieve formerly a flame
of Mr R. Ainslie's—company—Miss Jacky Grieve an amiable
sister of Mrs Thomson's and Mr Hood an honest, worthy,
facetious farmer in the neighbourhood—

Friday [*May 18*]—ride to Berwick— An idle town, but
rudely picturesque— Meet Lord Errol in walking round
the walls—his Lordship's flattering notice of me—dine with
Mr Clunzie Merch^t—nothing particular in company or conversation—come up a bold shore & over a wild country to
Eyemouth—sup & sleep at Mr Grieve's—

Saturday [*May 19*]—spend the day at Mr Grieve's— Made a
royal arch Mason of S^t. Ebbe's Lodge—Mr Wm Grieve, the
eldest brother, a joyous, warm-hearted, jolly, clever fellow—
takes a hearty glass & sings a good song—Mr Robt his
brother and partner in trade a good fellow but says little—
M^r [*name left blank*] Schoolmaster, of the partie an agre-

able fellow—take a sail after dinner—fishing of all kinds pays tithes at Eyemouth—

Sunday [*May 20*]—A Mr Robinson, a Brewer at Ednam sets out with us for Dunbar—

The Miss Grieves very good girls—My Bardship's heart got a brush from Miss Betsy—

Mr Willm Grieve's attachment to the family-circle so fond that when he is out, which by the by is often the case, he cannot go to bed till he see if all his sisters are sleeping well—pass the famous Abbey of Coldingham & Pease bridge —call at M^r. Sherriff's where M^r. A— & I dine—M^r. S— a talkative, conceited Idiot—I talk of love to Nancy all the evening while her brother escorts home some companions like himself— Sir James Hall of Dunglass having heard of my being in the neighbourhood comes to Mr Sheriff's to breakfast—takes me to see his fine scenery on the stream of Dunglass—Dunglas[s] the most romantic sweet place I ever saw—Sir James & his lady a pleasant happy couple—Sir James shows me a favorite spot beneath an oak where Lady Helen used to ponder on her lover Sir James being then abroad—he points out likewise a walk for which he has an uncommon respect as it was made by an Aunt of his to whom he owed much— Miss—[*sic*] will accompany me to Dunbar by way of making a parade of me as a sweetheart of hers among her relations—she mounts an old cart horse as huge and as lean as a house, a rusty old side saddle without girth or stirrup but fastened on with an old pillion girth—herself as fine as hands could make her in cream colored riding clothes, hat & feather, &c. I, ashamed of my situation, ride like the devil and almost shake her to pieces on old Jolly—get rid of her by refusing to call at her uncle's with her—

Past thro' the most glorious corn country I ever saw till

I reach Dunbar a neat little town—dine with Provost Fall an eminent Mercht. and most respectable character but undescribable as he [has no *(deleted)*] exhibits no marked traits—Mrs. Fall a genius in painting, fully more clever in the fine arts & sciences then [*sic*] my friend Lady Wauchope without her consummate assurance of her own abilities— Call with Mr Robinson (who, by the by, I find to be a worthy much respected man, very modest, warm, social heart which with less good sense than his would be perhaps with the children of prim precision & pride rather inimacal to that respect which is man's due from man) with him I call at on Miss Clarke, a maiden, in the Scotch phrase, "Guid enough but no brent new," a clever woman, with tolerable pretensions to remark and wit; while Time had blown the blushing bud of bashful modesty into the full-bosomed flower of easy confidence— She wanted to see what sort of raree show an Author was; and to let him know that though Dunbar was but a little town yet it was not destitute of people of parts.—

Breakfast next morning [*May 22*] at Skateraw, a Mr Lee's, a farmer of great note—Mr Lee an excellent, hospitable, social fellow, rather oldish, warm-hearted & chatty—a most judicious sensible farmer— Mr Lee detains me till next [day *(deleted)*] morning [*May 23*]—comp. at dinner— my revd acquaintance Dr Bowmaker, a revd., rattling, drunken old fellow—two sea Lieutenants; a Mr D. Lee, a cousin of the Landlord's, a fellow whose looks are of that kind which deceived me in a gentleman at Kelso, and has often deceived me; a goodly, handsome figure and face which incline one to give them credit for parts which they have not—Mr Clarke, a much cleverer fellow, but whose looks a little cloudy and his appearance rather ungainly, [make rather *(deleted)*] with an every-day Observer may prejudice the opinion against him— D^r. Brown, a medical young Gent. from Dunbar, a fellow whose face & manner are open and engaging— Leave Skateraw for Dunse next day along with Collector Lorimer, a lad of slender abilities and bashfully diffident to an extreme—

Found Miss Ainslie, the amiable, the sensible, the good-humored, the sweet Miss Ainslie all alone at Berrywell— Heavenly Powers who know the weaknesses of human hearts support mine! what happiness must I see only to remind me that I cannot enjoy it!

Lammermuir hills from East Lothian to Dunse, very wild— Dine with the Farmer's club at Kelso.— Sir Jno Hume & Mr Lamsden there but nothing worth remembering when the following circumstance is considered—I walk in to Dunse before dinner, & out to Berrywell in the evening with Miss Ainslie—how well-bred, how frank, how good she is! I could grasp her with rapture on a bed of straw, and rise with contentment to the most sweltering drudgery of stiffening Labor!

[Thursday *(deleted)*]—M^r. Kerr & I set out for to dine at Mr Hood's on our way to England—

Charming Rachel! may thy bosom never be wrung by the evils of this life of sorrows, or by the villainy of this world's sons!

I am taken extremely ill with strong feverish symptoms, & take a servant of Mr Hood's to watch me all night—embittering Remorse scares my fancy at the gloomy forebodings of death—I am determined to live for the future in such a manner as not to be scared at the approach of Death—I am sure I could meet him with indifference, but for "The Something beyond the grave"— M^r. Hood agrees to accompany us to England if we will wait him till Sunday—

[Thursday *(deleted)*]
Friday [*May 25*]

I go with Mr Hood to see the roup of an unfortunate Farmer's stock—rigid Economy & decent Industry, do you preserve me from being the principal Dramatis Persona in such a scene of horrors! Meet my good old friend M^r. Ainslie who calls on mr Hood in the evening to take farewel of my Bardship—this day I feel myself warm w^t. sentiments of gratitude to the Great Preserver of men who has kindly restored me to health and strength once more— A pleasant walk with my young friend Douglas Ainslie, a sweet, modest, clever young fellow—

Saturday [*May 26*]

ride out with Mr Hood to see the curiosities at Mr Swinton's, his Landlord—fine collection of Persian & other Oriental paintings, Boydell's Prints, &c.—

Sunday—27th May

Cross Tweed an[d] traverse the moors thro' a wild country till I reach Alnwick—Alnwick castle, a seat of the Duke of Northumberland, furnished in a most princely manner— A Mr Wilkin, an Agent of His Grace's, shows us the house & policies—M^r W— a discreet, sensible, ingenious man—

Monday [*May 28*]—

Come, still through byways, [to] Warworth [*sic*] where we dine—hermitage & old castle— Warkworth situated very picturesque with Coquet Island, a small rocky spot the seat of an old monastery, facing it a little in the sea; and the small but romantic river Coquet running through it— Sleep at Morpeth a pleasant little town, and on next day to Newcastle— Meet with a very agreable, sensible fellow, a M^r. Chattox, a Scotchman, who shows us a great many civilities and who dines & sups with us—

[Tuesday *(deleted)*]

[The following entries, printed by Cunningham, are not now with the MS]

Wednesday [*May 30*]—Left Newcastle early in the morning, and rode over a fine country to Hexham to breakfast—from Hexham to Wardrue, the celebrated Spa, where we slept.

Thursday [*May 31*]—Reach Longtown to dine, and part there with my good friends Messrs Hood and Ker.— A hiring day in Longtown.— I am uncommonly happy to see so many young folks enjoying life.— I come to Carlisle. (Meet a strange enough romantic adventure by the way, in falling in with a girl and her married sister—the girl, after some overtures of gallantry on my side, sees me a little cut with the bottle, and offers to take me in for a Gretna-green affair. I, not being quite such a gull as she imagines, make an appointment with her, by way of vive la bagatelle, to hold a conference on it when we reach town.— I meet her in town and give her a brush of caressing and a bottle of cyder; but finding herself un peu trompée in her man, she sheers off.) Next day [*June 1*] I meet my good friend, Mr Mitchell, and walk with him round the town and its environs, and through his printing-works, &c.—four or five hundred people employed, many of them women and children.— Dine with Mr Mitchell, and leave Carlisle.— Come by the coast to Annan.— Overtaken on the way by a curious old fish of a shoemaker, and miner from Cumberland mines.

["Here," says Cunningham, "the Manuscript abruptly ends." It contains, however, the following miscellaneous notes:]

Kilmarnock 15th [June?] 1787 Recd. from Mr Robt. Muir eleven pounds ten shillings Sterl. to acct of copies of my book sent to him.—

Do from Do on same acct one pound five shillings

Do from Do on same acct two pounds ten shillings

To Miss F[errier]

[Nae heathen I here *(deleted)*]
Nae heathen name shall I prefix
    O' gentry frae Parnassus;
Auld Reekie dings them a' to sticks
    For rhyme-inspiring lasses—

Tune, Duncan Davison

There was a lass they ca'd her Meg
The brawest lass in a' the town
And mony a lad her love did beg
Thro' a' the country round and round

[*Here follows what is apparently the first draft of the elegy* On the Death of Sir James Hunter Blair. *The greater part of the first and second stanzas, and the whole of the tenth, are written in ink; the remainder, in pencil, is almost completely illegible.*]

Glasgow 1ˢᵗ. April 1778 G. Arms. Spiers, Mur. & Co. Nº $\frac{17}{107}$

Dº Thistle bank $\overline{294}$ 2ᵈ Aug: 1783
these two five £ notes sent by post to my brother
[*A page of illegible penciled memoranda follows*]
James Hog, Shoemaker, Buchanan's Land, head of the Cannongate—
Miss Russell Nº 20 Great Mary le bon London
Mem. To enquire for a Mʳ Clarke, Rector of a grammar School somewhere about Saltcoats or Irvine
Direct for Dʳ Moore To Major Moore M.P. Clifford Street, Burlington Gardens—
Jas. Candlish—at Mʳˢ Barrs first land above the Crosswell Glasgow [*Not in Burns' hand.*]

We'll aiblins get a flyte and aiblins nane
We'll say it was fan ye fell o'er the stane
And hurt sae sair as coudna rise your lane!

Memorandum—to write out the preceeding part of this Poem for Mrs Fall—Dunbar.

Whitelaw 3 miles from Haddington 7 miles from Dunbar 250 p^r. Annum

Willm Lumsden W.S. Apply to

19 miles from Ed^r. 1 mile from Leably Sinclair

Edin^r August 14th 1787

Payed to Mr Miers for two profiles on account of Mr Aiken, Ayr, 15 sh. —————————

Whope, a glen between two hills—

Parreck, to force a ewe to Mother an alien lamb by closing them up together—

INDEX

INDEX

DATE DUE